223820

725.21

"RELATING TO THE COMMON MAN

IN AN UNCOMMON WAY IS THE GOAL."

JON JERDE

Phaidon Press Limited
Regent's Wharf
All Saints Street
London N1 9PA

First published 1999
© 1999 Phaidon Press Limited
Free Pass at Heaven's Gate © 1999 Ray
Bradbury

ISBN 0 7148 3830 6

A CIP catalogue record for this book is
available from the British Library.

Printed in Hong Kong

YOU ARE HERE

The Jerde Partnership International

Transformative projects occur in built-up areas in inner cities and suburbs, which have been blighted or fallen into decline. They can revitalize such neighborhoods, taking architectural cues from the existing and surrounding environments and transforming their previous identity. These interventions often act as catalysts for economic growth and social regeneration in the surrounding area.

Formative projects occupy areas of unbuilt land, both inside and outside of cities and suburbs. Conceptually, they may be inspired by their surroundings, but do not take direct visual cues from this environment, tending to be self-contained projects; a world-within-a-world that forms a new and distinct identity for the location. Like the transformative projects, the new development can effect economic and social regeneration at its edges.

Free Pass at Heaven's Gate Ray Bradbury

There is, I recall, an Egyptian myth about passing muster, getting through, being allowed entrance, at Heaven's Gate. Arriving there at some far future date, you will be asked just one question by the God of the Dead.

Did you have enthusiasm?

If the answer is Yes! You're in!

Which brings us to Jon Jerde.

Enthusiasm?

His answer would blow the ears off that dread Egyptian God.

Another Egyptian metaphor applies here. The pharaohs, buried with bread and onions for the trip, were accompanied by pedestrian slaves or boatmen. If their children died, toys were stashed in their tombs so the gods would come play.

Jerde, in his fevers, puts toys, immense toys, not in our tombs, but out front, in back, topside and bottom, of our lives. So *we* can come play.

Most architects ignore or bore us with their conceptual ennui, gum our eyes shut with banalities.

Jerde jars us awake and alert, with his lively sense of fun and beauty, a fused mixture that keeps us off balance. One glance at his out-size toys makes us *want to go in*!

Jon Jerde arrived in my life almost twenty years ago. We were introduced by John DeCuir Jr., a superb designer of motion picture sets. At lunch, Jerde said,

"Have you seen Glendale Galleria? What do you think of it?"

"It's great."

"It's yours!" said Jerde. "I followed the blueprint you sketched in the *L.A. Times* two years ago, designing a mall with all its proper human components."

"Am I allowed to say that?" I said.

"Why?" said Jerde.

"Because." I said, "I want to be able to claim you as my bastard son."

And thus began one of the happiest years of my life. Jon invited me and DeCuir Jr. to join him one or two days a week at seven in the morning, an ungodly hour for me, but a wild and fascinating hour for all of us. We threw conversational confetti to the air and ran under to see how much each of us caught. We blueprinted cities, malls and museums by the triple dozen, threw them on the floor, stepped on them, and birthed more with all three gabbing at once. I felt honoured to be allowed in as an amateur Palladio with my meager experience but Futurist hopes.

Many years ago, François Truffaut, that fine French film director, came to visit. What, I said to my wife, do we do to enchant this director from the most beautiful city in the world?

Maggie and I took Truffaut high up on the Hollywood Hills where you could see *our* City of Light. Four hundred square miles of metropolitan illumination, a vast seascape of electricity. Then before he could regain his breath, we raced him downhill to the confectionery confines of the Piggly Wiggly Continental, the most sublime outcrop of the American genus Super Market. This was 1960 and the supermarket had not yet invaded France. The Piggly Wiggly Continental, like its name, was a wild meld of sophisticated wines and spirits, Jolly Green Giant vegetables and a reinvented Five and Dime store. Truffaut ran amok in the shopping jungle.

All this is a preliminary to Jon Jerde and Medici and Boticelli remembrances.

During a period of employment at Disney's Imagineering studio I invited Jon out to prowl this rest home for hidden Renaissance sculptors and artists. Save that they were *not* resting but thriving. Anything you might want, saved up from lost time, could be found and summoned back to life here by the sons of the sons of the sons of Da Vinci, Bellini and Michelangelo.

If Jon Jerde's hair did not stand on end, it bristled; if cold chills did not ripple his neck, I imagined them. He became Truffaut at the Piggly Wiggly, a dog glad to see its master after being long away. He moved faster than I could in this sublime territory. Time does not have to die, it all said. Fashions do not have to go out of fashion. Palladio only *seems* dead, sound his alarm clock. Goya and Klee gone? Still *here*! Sir John Soane's Museum in London, with its Piranesis and Hogarths still alive alive-o? Turn left, then right, in Imagineering.

At the end of the tour I was exhausted, Jon was fevering his second wind. He was almost prepared to sign up with the Mouse.

It never happened. Which is just as well. His brush with Imagineering made me recall a lunch with Disney when he was conceptualizing Tomorrowland. I suggested he hire me to help rebuild.

"It's no use, Ray," Walt said. "You're a genius, I'm a genius. We'd kill each other the first week."

So it was just as well Jon took other roads with no names and numbers, and traveled light.

I was delighted to travel with him for a few hours each week so many years ago. I recall two incidences, one bad, one good, to illustrate how Jerde works.

I sat with Jon when the Baltimore Power Plant people asked him to reconceive their waterfront property. With John DeCuir Jr. we came up with some wild Jules Verne, H.G. Wells twenty-first cum nineteenth century concepts. At a board meeting with the Baltimore and some Six Flags people we felt our bright flags being torn, our Montgolfier balloons pricked and our submarine run aground. We needed fifty million dollars to start. The Power Plant people had birthed a midget twenty-nine million, hardly enough to turn on the lights. It was time to leave. Jon gave the nod to DeCuir and myself, and we were gone. The Power Plant, rejuvenated on the cheap, opened a few years later, and collapsed.

The obvious point is Jerde does not hitchhike any notion that comes down the pipe. He is not running to the bank, but to the drawing board.

A happier instance was Jerde's being asked to bring downtown San Diego back from the dead. Jon asked me to write a blueprint essay from which to take off. I wrote 'The Aesthetics of Lostness.' One of the great joys of travel, I said, was being lost in a great city and loving it. If Jon could build his Plaza on the principle of being lost and safe and filled with joy, that would be splendid. Jon did just that. Standing outside Horton Plaza looking in you say, "Yeah, Gangway! I want to be lost!" My input: one percent. Jon and his team's input: ninety-nine percent.

Perfection.

To sum up: Albert Schweitzer, that good African medic once said, do something good, someone may imitate it. Jerde is his good acolyte student.

What he has created, let no cynic put asunder. His colony of ideas has caused some few super-doubters who disgruntle his beauties, hate his cleanliness and recant his changing old times for new. Do not be an architectural Cézanne, they cry, with your fruit bowl rearranging the garbage. There's nothing wrong with tossed cigarette butts, used Kleenex and fish-wrapped gutter tabloids.

But Jerde's response is he never met an abandoned downtown slum he didn't love. Love to re-do, of course. Get it to take nourishment, sit up, stand, walk and then win the Olympics.

Some mornings I wake at that ungodly seven o'clock hour, and wish I were running with him still.

Urban Transformations Frances Anderton

You Are Here

You are in the midst of a crowd of people meandering through lively streets, alleys and open piazzas. On all sides are stores, cinemas and cafes, in vivid buildings with dazzling signs; around you are colorful stalls and push-carts, fountains and trees. There is a cacophony of sounds emanating from all directions; there are mime artists and street performers. It's chaotic, vibrant and loud. Where are you? You are in public space, Jerde-style.

These are places where fantasy, commerce, entertainment and public life have merged. They include shops, parks, cinemas, perhaps a theme park, a sports arena, housing, a casino, a public amphitheatre, a new canal or forest—maybe all of the above. They are owned sometimes by one company, or a consortium, or a public/private partnership. These mixed-use developments represent a movement in architecture and city-making today far more significant than the latest boutique restaurant or avant-garde art gallery. They represent a new twist on an old art—the making of a civic realm.

Prominent examples of this new type of public space are Horton Plaza, Universal CityWalk and Mall of America in the USA, **Beursplein** in Rotterdam, Canal City Hakata in Fukuoka, Japan. These are all brazen, commercial places that the public loves and critics love to debate, and they are all designed by LA-based architect and urbanist Jon Jerde, with his firm, the Jerde Partnership International.

Jon Jerde, who considers himself to be a "place-maker," is a darling of developers and city managers and a challenge to the cultural élite. Armed with rare talents—among them, an understanding of the ability of the retail program to support his social and architectural vision—Jerde has taken the most maligned building type, the shopping center, and

has helped to transform it into a public venue that has in turn transformed **urban centers** and **suburbs** from Los Angeles to Rotterdam to Tokyo.

But while shopping may have been his medium, the message is community. Jerde's goal is to bring people together—to restore urban vitality to cities and suburbs denuded by zoning of land-use, neglected by civic leaders and by architects' indifference to popular taste. The commercial realm has offered the means to do that—firstly with shops, and subsequently with sports facilities and casinos, with urban parks and now housing developments. Having started as a shopping center designer, Jerde has gone on to become a veritable alchemist of the urban condition, hired to analyze the decline of a street, a neighborhood, a city and to devise site-specific strategies to kick-start them back into life. *You Are Here* is a process of discovery: about Jon Jerde, his firm, his vision and the evolution of his controversial work from shopping center maverick of the 1970s to creator of "third millennium cities."[1] It is about defining our surroundings at the beginning of the twenty-first century.

Horton Plaza

It all started in 1977, when the developer Ernest Hahn was persuaded by the city's visionary mayor to build a shopping center in downtown San Diego. The location, an abandoned six-block site near the waterfront, was a textbook example of an ailing American downtown. Hahn hired Jon Jerde, then in self-imposed retirement from a frustrating ten years of shopping center design, as architect. For Jerde, here at last was the chance to "make the ordinary, extraordinary." It was the long awaited opportunity to test ideas that had been fomenting for over a decade. It was Jerde's chance to transform a

shopping center into a "conscious creation of human urbanism."[2]

Jerde tells a story about how he and his team of designers worked feverishly for days and nights creating a theatrical model of pasted card and poster paint. "After the experience-making team got done, the upholstery team came in and glued on the architecture, then came the team that made little bake sales to imply life in this place … then we put everybody in black turtlenecks and hand held spotlights. It was very corny and very dramatic."[3] Once ready, they literally raised the curtain and stunned their audience of developers and city officials with a six-block profusion of shops, restaurants, outdoor theater and cinema, housed in exuberant Spanish, Moorish and Italian Renaissance-styled buildings, with parapets, balconies and towers, stairways, elevators and bridges teeming with people.

It took three days, he says, before any of the witnesses to this spectacle found the words to respond but when they did it was with unanimous approval. Horton Plaza was built just like the model—even to the point of being constructed of inexpensive, painted stucco structures—and opened in 1985. It was anticipated that it would take five years before **Horton Plaza** made a financial return, but it was an instant success, garnering 25 million visitors in the first year. Even more significantly, Horton Plaza became such a magnet that the blighted waterfront surroundings and nearby historic district were also redeveloped, with new housing and offices, a convention center and light railway. San Diego's downtown had returned from the dead, and Jon Jerde and his office, The Jerde Partnership International, was launched.

Suburban Los Angeles, California, USA.

Downtown Los Angeles, California, USA.

Beursplein, Rotterdam, The Netherlands.

Horton Plaza, San Diego, California, USA, gala opening.

Horton Plaza, San Diego, California, USA.

At Horton Plaza, the Jerde Partnership took the conventional regional mall formula—shops and cinemas anchored by four department stores and parking garages—sited it in an urban setting, recon-figured the parts, and spiced them up with theaters and specialty shops, food courts and party ambiance (typical of the festival centers popu-larized in the 1970s). By connecting the internal "armature"—the focal double-curved diagonal street slashing through the project—with the existing downtown streets, they reversed the industry prototype of what Jerde describes as "the insulated, introspective box operating in a surrounding field of automobiles."[4] In addition, they created something distinct, a new element: entertaining architecture. The design was picturesque rather than rationalist, seemingly chaotic rather than orderly, and cinematic in its kinetic feel and stagy evocation of fantasy Latin America. This was no formulaic dumbell-plan suburban mall; it was an experience. Goodbye retail, hello "experiential" design.[5]

Horton Plaza was opened a year after the 1984 **Los Angeles Olympic Games**, also designed by the Jerde Partnership, with environmental graphic designers Sussman/Prezja and a team of graphic designers, artists and architects. The brilliantly effective visual identity of the Olympics—a cata-logue of parts of inexpensive, brightly colored fabrics and shapes linking sports events across the 1,000 square mile Los Angeles region—stunned local residents and the rest of the world. The success of both projects was such that Jerde was hailed by developers and politicians as a miracle-worker, uniquely capable of reversing a seemingly irre-versible decline of commercial centers, even cities. The Jerde Partnership was established in 1977 and

has gone on to design numerous retail and multi-use complexes. Some are variations on similar themes, but others have been innovative concepts that have shaped retail development and urban regeneration. Among them, **CityWalk**, the model for what became known as the Urban Entertainment Center; **Mall of America**, an enormous enclosed theme park surrounded by shops in the ultimate fusing of theming and retail; **The Fremont Street Experience**, five blighted blocks in downtown Las Vegas recast as a "destination experience"; and **Canal City Hakata**, a multiuse commercial complex that sets the current benchmark for large-scale private retail development.

The *New York Times* pronounced Horton Plaza "the most important shopping mall to be built in any American downtown…" since the festival marketplace.[6] The design for the LA Olympics was universally admired. Yet, despite this notable acclaim, Jon Jerde has since had a mixed reception. Critics have accused him of parodying traditional public space and the vitality of communal expe-rience. CityWalk is "probably the most insidious kind of theme park," charged polemical urban critic Mike Davis at its opening.[7] "Architecture as packaging or playacting, as disengagement from reality, is a notion whose time, alas, seems to have come," mourned Ada Louise Huxtable about the theming of America, with which she associates Jon Jerde.[8] He has been painted as responsible for transforming the real into ersatz, and retail into a religion; and accused of being a master salesman masquerading as a guru of city-making, peddling a clever spin on an old building type. The architectural press has tended to treat him as an outsider, seeing him as a shopping center designer, and someone who reviled the basic tenets of Modernism, preferring narrative

collages of buildings and public spaces to isolated object-buildings. Jerde describes his concern with "the bottom 40 feet" of a building, because that is "the people part," i.e., the level where people walk, sit, make eye contact, engage with stores, cafes and businesses.

Jerde's form of city-building is not everyone's cup of tea. His projects to date have tended to meld the postmodern narrative or "experiential" (some would call it themed) space, with an often hyper-stimulatory bombardment of synthetic franchise stores, lights, vivid signs, music, street performers, push-cart vendors and jostling people. But there is no question that such places are incredibly popular with the public and therefore with developers and city managers. It is also true that they are very inventive—even the venerable Huxtable was compelled to admit that CityWalk was "witty and sophisticated."[9] Jerde's projects are built on a scale beyond belief, growing beyond the boundaries of city blocks. Mall of America, at 4.2 million square feet, is the largest shopping center in the USA; Canal City Hakata comprises 2.5 million square feet (and has its own canal); The Fremont Street Experience is five blocks in length; Horton Plaza six blocks. In projects in development, twelve square blocks is typical. Add to that the emergence in the 1990s of entertainment-based shopping and leisure environments, coupled with the prevailing retreat from suburban planning, and Jerde's form of place-making is not only fascinating but an essential subject of study.

A critical shift to this view is now taking place. Many observers are reevaluating Jerde as a genuine populist who has skillfully harnessed the forces of our time to reinvigorate cities and create human-scaled, exciting places for the masses. Architect

Universal CityWalk, Universal City, California, USA.

Mall of America, Bloomington, Minnesota, USA.

The Fremont Street Experience, Las Vegas, Nevada, USA.

Canal City Hakata, Fukuoka, Japan.

Los Angeles Olympic Games, Los Angeles, California, USA.

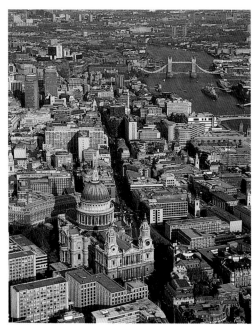

Rem Koolhaas, who is himself tackling the same problems of scale and mass culture, lectures on Jon Jerde's role in the retail industry, as part of an architectural thesis program at Harvard University Graduate School of Design. And one of the princelings of high art architecture, Arata Isozaki, recently pronounced Canal City Hakata one of the most important pieces of architecture of the late 1990s.

The other building Isozaki cited, incidentally, was the **Guggenheim Museum** in Bilbao, Spain, by Frank Gehry. Gehry is a friend of Jon Jerde, and fellow University of Southern California alumnus who similarly started out in and broke free of retail and commercial architecture. Now, at the end of the twentieth century, those two designers from Los Angeles—ground zero, the anticity, the ultimate suburb—have become world leaders in their respective fields. Each draws inspiration from nature, organic forms and popular culture.

The time is ripe, if not overdue, therefore, for a comprehensive survey of the Jerde Partnership's work. With a foreword by Ray Bradbury, essays by three Los Angeles-based writers, architectural historian Margaret Crawford, cultural critic Norman M. Klein and architect Craig Hodgetts, descriptions of the firm's most significant projects, and excerpts of Jerde's own philosophy, this book illustrates the evolution of the firm's work over two decades.

Cities in Transition

Jerde's work marks the end of a century that has witnessed a change in cities from the nineteenth-century industrial model—concentrated, vertical, public transit- and pedestrian-based (New York, Paris, **London**)—to the postwar, postindustrial, automobile-dependent, sprawling, multicentered

model like Los Angeles and the fast-growing sunbelt cities. As we enter the twenty-first century, with rapid population growth (California alone is projected to almost double its current population to approximately 60 million by 2040), the cityscape is mutating into a confusing hybrid of the two. Sprawling cities like **Los Angeles** are becoming more urban while older cities are becoming decentered and ringed by increasingly dense suburbs that have been christened by Norman M. Klein as "metropolitan suburbs." Retail has kept pace with, at times even led, these changes, as explored in greater depth by Margaret Crawford in her essay, "The Architect and the Mall."

Commerce began its exodus from auto-congested downtowns in the 1920s, first with small strip malls, then larger shopping centers on the edges of big cities. In the 1950s, regional malls boomed in tandem with postwar suburban development and population growth, reaching their zenith in the early 1970s. In 1972 there were 13,174 shopping centers in the United States, all of them versions of a generic planning and financing formula agreed upon by lenders, insurance companies, department store executives and major tenants. At that time the rearguard action set in. In the late 1960s and '70s, architects, planners and citizens, galvanized by activist Jane Jacobs and her book *The Death and Life of Great American Cities*,[10] began attempts to save downtowns through piecemeal gentrification. And in 1976, the first "**festival marketplace**," the Rouse Company's Faneuil Hall in Boston, Massachusetts, designed by Benjamin Thompson & Associates, was built.

But resistance efforts by community groups and planners were outpaced by out-of-town shopping centers, which grew faster and bigger

than ever in the 1980s; there were 16,000 built in the USA between 1980 and 1990. This was an era that welcomed the "superregional" center, a mall larger than 800,000 square feet. Only the recession in the early 1990s slowed progress, redirecting efforts towards the remodeling and expansion of now-decaying regional malls. Coupled with the decrease of federal investment in public space and the increased dependence of cities on sales tax (in the United States), this has led to the growth of two phenomena: the out-of-town, unadorned, complexes of discount stores, known as "power centers," and the revitalization of both downtowns and suburban centers by means of privately developed, entertainment-based malls, known as Urban Entertainment Centers.

The Urban Entertainment Center, or UEC, was a hybrid of entertainment, retailing and leisure, often in a themed environment, that developed in the early 1990s. It was a response to the assault on single-purpose "products"—shopping, sport, hospitality—from alternative forms of leisure and of distribution, such as movies, TV, theme parks and video arcades, the Internet, direct mail and wholesale outlets. It exploited the mass merchandizing potential of the brand identities of theme parks and cinemas (Disney, Warner, Universal, for example). UEC is often given as the umbrella title for destinations ranging from themed restaurants, such as Planet Hollywood, The Fashion Café, The Sports Café and the **Hard Rock Café**, to so-called "category killer" cinema complexes (totaling up to 40 or 50 screens). Entertainment-linked retailing, sports stadiums and stores, and themed casino/hotel complexes in Las Vegas have also been described as Urban Entertainment Centers.

While their genesis can be traced back to

Frank O. Gehry & Associates, Guggenheim Museum, Bilbao, Spain. Aerial view of London, UK.

Aerial view of Los Angeles, California, USA. Benjamin Thompson & Associates, Faneuil Hall and Marketplace, Boston, Massachusetts, USA.

Hard Rock Café, Los Angeles, California, USA.

Disneyland, with its romanticized, themed attractions such as Adventureland, Frontierland and the all-American Main Street, their arrival on the urban scene was arguably heralded by the 1993 opening of **CityWalk** at Universal City in Los Angeles, a bustling, faux-LA "street" of specialty stores and cafes.

While they predominated in Southern California, in the 1990s the descendants of UECs have spread worldwide. A popular destination for residents of Budapest, Hungary, for example, is Duna Plaza, a shopping and entertainment center featuring an indoor ice rink and nine movie screens, and the first of many more malls planned for that city. Such centers are springing up on defunct industrial sites and in the suburbs of old cities in Europe and Asia. They have been touted by developers and city managers from Times Square to Tokyo as the panacea for declining downtowns and suburban shopping centers, signaling the future for public recreation. Many of the top corporate firms in America, such as RTKL Associates (who designed the 1996 Centro Oberhausen in Oberhausen, Germany, and the new "**Printworks**" in Manchester, UK), Hellmuth Obata Kassabaum (HOK) and Gensler Associates (responsible for **Sony Theatres** Lincoln Square in New York) have moved into entertainment-based design in the 1990s. So have the in-house design teams of movie companies and small design practices in Los Angeles. Of the top ten architectural firms in Los Angeles,[11] six were working on entertainment-related projects.

These developments have been so successful that their lead has been followed elsewhere, with managers employing similar moves—pedestrianization, anchoring multiplexes, landscaping, street performers, sidewalk cafes and so on—to turn around declining commercial strips. Third Street Promenade in Santa Monica, California (created by the City of Santa Monica in partnership with Third Street merchants in 1989), is just one example of a stunningly successful renewal of a defunct downtown by these means.

The transforming of the street into a pedestrianized destination, however, suggests that while this may seem to denote the return of foot traffic and communality to a car-dependent, alienating environment, it does so only in a circumscribed place. In many, particularly suburban, locations, people still have to drive or travel there in order to walk. Some critics argue that **Horton Plaza** and its progeny are essentially the old suburban model, providing the new experience of traditional urbanity. But without their additional social and urban goals, would they still function as retail centers that successfully attract a captive audience?

Third Millennium Cities

In Jerde's case, however, he is designing site-specific solutions, not the now generic UEC. He rejects the label and argues that the public's appetite for what are essentially cynically jazzed-up versions of the standardized retail center will be short-lived.

Furthermore, the Jerde Partnership is building not only shopping centers, but rather, what the firm terms third millennium cities. Horton Plaza, CityWalk, **Canal City Hakata**, and the variations on these projects, have been just staging posts on an evolutionary journey towards creating "the appropriate vessel for a renaissance of the human communal scene."[12]

Since most of the Jerde Partnership's work has been for shopping center or commercial developers, Jerde has had to create public, civic space in the commercial, private realm. But his ambition is to create new, multiuse urban cores with all the attributes of a real city—commercial, residential, retail, entertainment and public space.

Cities have lost their souls, believes Jerde, by segregating their uses. In postwar cities, housing and sports venues and office centers and shops were not only zoned but created by specialist financiers and developers who knew nothing of the other building types. Jerde realized that successful public places integrated the uses—to accomplish this, the "housing guys, the office guys, the retail guys, the sports guys and the finance guys"[13] would have to harness their efforts.

As city councils, developers and mayors worldwide take an increasing interest in the Jerde Partnership's work, the firm is beginning to realize these dreams. On the drawing boards are designs for large urban neighborhoods—**Dentsu Headquarters at Shiodome**, Namba, and **Roppongi 6-6** in Japan, One Reeperbahn in Hamburg, new downtowns for ailing middle American cities such as Kansas City and Salt Lake City. Where Jerde schemes have, to date, mostly excluded the car from the environment, these new projects will include thoroughfares. Where the Jerde projects have hitherto provided for a few hours of entertainment, these multiuse places will have entertainment at the core, while functioning twenty-four hours a day.

It will be the new century before such projects are completed, but Canal City Hakata marks a large step in this direction. An example of Jerde's work at its most confident and successful, Canal City Hakata, opened in 1996, is a complex of offices, hotels, stores, theaters and public spaces organized along a meandering canal. It is a design that synthesizes local and global influences and also emphasises the predominant preoccupations in

Universal CityWalk, Universal City, California, USA.

RTKL Associates, "Printworks," Manchester, UK.

Gensler Associates, Sony Theatres, New York,
New York, USA.

Horton Plaza, San Diego, California, USA.

Canal City Hakata, Fukuoka, Japan.

Dentsu Headquarters at Shiodome, Tokyo, Japan.

Roppongi 6-6, Tokyo, Japan.

Jerde's work: the infusion of landscaping into the manmade environment.

Nature and the Cosmos
The aim in the Jerde Partnership's work has been to infuse many elements into its projects, with the creation of dynamic public space always the main goal. In the earlier projects the retail program was fused with entertainment and experiential design. In more recent projects nature and allusions to the cosmos have become a larger part of the mix. "We've hit the end of that chapter," says Jerde, in reference to urbanistic projects like CityWalk. Projects such as Namba, in Osaka, Japan, a huge urban parkscape concealing retail underground, "represent the beginning of the new one."[14]

With a shortage of US-based work in the late 1980s and early '90s due to an economic recession, Jerde's prescient partner, Eddie Wang, cultivated work in Asia. It was there, in Taiwan, Indonesia and, especially, Japan, that the firm found tremendous receptiveness to ideas that, Jerde believes, American investors would not then have supported. Perhaps with their traditions of Zen Buddhism, Shintoism and neo-Confucianism, the Japanese are, as Charles Jencks argues, "more open to the metaphysics of contemporary science than those in the West, where there is a protracted war between Christianity and Modern Science."[15] Perhaps also because of the opening of borders to foreign influence after centuries of seclusion, coupled with the country's sudden prosperity and its cramping density, Japan has embraced **eclectic, hyperreal and artificial environments**. Such places range from the architecture of Branson Coates, **Itsuko Hasegawa** and **Shin Takamatsu** to the ubiquitous artificial ski slopes and golf ranges. In this atmos-phere Jon Jerde was given a green light to go cosmic.

The firm has designed a string of urban renewal and leisure projects, in various stages of development, which explore ideas about man's relationship to nature and Gaia, cultural differences and the marriage of East and West. Makuhari Town Center, designed for the new town of Makuhari, is a microcosm of the earth, inside a sphere inside a cube: Rokko Island, Shiodome, Roppongi and Rinku Town are all urban renewal plans in which highly picturesque landscaping is the glue for the office buildings and shops. At Canal City Hakata, Jerde and his team, despite initial hesitation from locals (who associated canal water with sewers), inserted a new canal as the spine of the project; they created a canyon of undulating buildings inspired by Arizona's **Canyon de Chelly**; and they textured the cladding to appear as if it was growing from rustic and rough at the base, like a cliff-face, to smooth and industrial at the top—from primeval to manmade.

The Journey
Jerde considers himself a creature of the globe. Both gregarious and a loner, he says, "I have never had any particular allegiance to any place, state, town or neighborhood. I have learned to like them all." While Jerde's work employs the heightened theatricality and narrative tricks of the movies, so his own life, as he tells it, is etched with the drama and dreams of old Hollywood. The only child of peripatetic parents, his father was an itinerant oil field engineer, building refineries—"Our family was called oil-field trash," he remembers, "we just blew into town and we blew out of town."[16] Jerde recounts a lonely childhood during which his passion, from an early age, was for building fantasy cities with the materials at hand: pipes, spheres, cylinders and tin sheds. On moving to Southern California as a child (aged about ten) he found a spiritual home at the **Long Beach Pike**, an early theme park in Long Beach, California. There he found "a wonderful warmth and sense of belonging among all these anonymous folks."[17] He came to understand that he was "addicted to communality, as long as it's anonymous."[18] This attitude expresses itself in the kinds of public spaces that, to quote historian J. B. Jackson, "draw people together and give them a momentary pleasure and sense of well-being."[19] These transitory spaces are not necessarily the ideal Aristotlean agora, or public square, that Jackson has written about, that would be purely "for the exchange of ideas."[20]

Jerde studied art and engineering for a year starting in 1957 at the University of California at Los Angeles (UCLA) then trained as an architect at the University of Southern California (USC), from 1959 to 1965. He received a BA in Architecture under the guidance of landscape designer, and then USC Dean, Emmet Wemple—a "very dear friend who taught me how to be humanistic!" recalls Jerde. Architectural and philosophical influences he cites are **Louis Sullivan**, **Frank Lloyd Wright**, Louis Kahn, and Paolo Soleri. To Jerde, each represented the antithesis of soulless Modernism. Sullivan's buildings, says Jerde, captured the "underlying idea of the organic," while "Wright's concept of the organic and what he did with it in terms of geometries was very exciting." And Kahn, "reintroduced the spiritual into architecture after a long cold march." Jerde was inspired almost more by Kahn's teachings than his buildings—"he talked," says Jerde, "about the life of a thing, with a heart and a liver and a kidney... then produced buildings that

Artificial ski slope, Japan.
Tokyo Dome, Tokyo, Japan.
Itsuko Hasegawa Atelier, Shonandai Cultural Center, Fujisawa, Japan.
Shin Takamatsu, Future Port City.

Canyon de Chelly, Arizona, USA.

Long Beach Pike, Long Beach, California, USA.
Louis Sullivan, Carson Pirie Scott Building, Chicago, Illinois, USA.
Frank Lloyd Wright, Guggenheim Museum, New York, New York, USA.

were antirational, or visceral."[21] But perhaps his most important influence was Paolo Soleri, the creator of Arcosanti, whom he met when he was fifteen years old, having been introduced by Soleri's assistant, Banks Upshore, a protégé of Bruce Goff. "I'd spend evenings at Soleri's drafting board, reading the tremendous notebooks he'd done." It was "not the shapes," the free-form concrete monoliths by the renegade builder-designer, that captivated him, "but the search for community at a gigantic scale."[22]

While at USC he painted and sculpted intensively, and steeped himself in the milieu and tenets of architectural Modernism, that he would later reject. In 1963 he won a year-long travel scholarship to Europe, which gave him his next formative experience, the discovery of the **Italian hill towns**, "made not 'by somebody' but 'by everybody.'"[23] He began to formulate a vision for places that would re-create the dense urbanity and collective creativity of the organic pre-Modernist hill towns, the communality and fun of popular amusement parks like Long Beach Pike, and the multiplicity of influences, manmade and natural, that had characterized his nomadic childhood.

On returning to Los Angeles, he established his own office but found himself propelled by economic necessity to take a corporate job. In 1967 he joined shopping center designers Burke, Kober, Nicolais, Archuleta (which became Charles Kober Associates in 1973) as design director, where he learned everything about and became depressed by the formulaic and soulless retail design of the time. He left in 1977 and went on a professional and educational odyssey, renovating old buildings and studying urban form. This journey took him to San Francisco, Seattle and Europe. When in Seattle he had what he

describes as "a totally transforming epiphany" about "the strength of 'is-ness'"[24] and the deep meaning of communality. He further concluded that "the consumption addiction is what will bring people out and together"[25] and that if he was to create the utopian public spaces that preoccupied him, he would have to do it with retail. Later, Ada Louise Huxtable would remark in her book that "… no one, from Tony Garnier to Patrick Geddes, knew that shopping would be the glue to hold it [utopia] together."[26] It was later the same year, when Jerde returned to Los Angeles, that he was approached by the retail developer Ernest Hahn, who took a leap of faith and invested in Jerde's ideas for Horton Plaza.

Jerde is driven, creative, persuasive, charming. Depending on who you talk to, he is inspired, but temperamental, prone to bouts of dark introspection and to high-spirited, childlike enthusiasm. Enter his inner sanctum and after a three-hour conversational odyssey through philosophy, psychotherapy, Eastern religion, futurism and the state of the cosmos, you feel seduced by his gurulike intensity. In meetings and public presentations, he wows listeners with a combination of shrewd understanding of the retail industry, infectious vision and lack of condescension. He embraces the zeitgeist and makes you want to come along for the ride. "You can't be around him describing a project without falling in love with him and the project," says Harry Usher, the Chief Operating Officer of the 1984 Olympics. Since wowing Usher and Ernest Hahn, Jerde has drawn many people into his orbit. Perhaps his most passionate collaboration was with science-fiction writer Ray Bradbury. In Bradbury, Jerde found a creative soulmate. Together they designed some other-worldly,

imaginary cities. Others are long-standing collaborators in his co-creative teams – in which Jerde brings together diverse talents of collaborators, consultants and clients and encourages them to develop their own visions within a shared overarching concept. This strategy, appropriate for the vast-scale projects the Jerde Partnership works on, results in "the artistry of choir-singing" rather than the stamp of "original authorship."[27] But for the choir to sing in harmony, Jerde is the concertmaster. The firm always works with associate architects and often with co-creative teams, but as design architect the Jerde Partnership develops the overall concept for the projects. The role it plays in the stages between concept design and completion varies with individual projects.

The Jerde Partnership International now numbers around 130 people, who are ensconced in a light, three-story office that opens directly onto the Venice boardwalk in Los Angeles. The boardwalk is a beachfront stretch of cheap shops, shabby apartment buildings and cafes, and daily sideshows: sword swallowers, chainsaw jugglers, dancing Rollerbladers, hemp activists and psychics, one-man-bands and pavement artists. It is the venue for a daily carnival of humans and canines of every race, age and appearance that parade up and down in a fabulous, sometimes freakish Southern California version of *passegiata*. The boardwalk provides an example of the type of spontaneous communal happening Jerde's designers are trying to generate.

Here in light, spacious rooms overlooking the boardwalk, teams work on different projects under the guidance of a project designer and, ultimately, Jerde himself, who holds meetings in his cavernous, richly hued office (located on the windowless, alley

Loreto Aprutino, Abruzzi, Italy.

Original watercolor artwork by Jon Jerde.
Staff at the Jerde Partnership International office, Venice
Beach, California, USA.

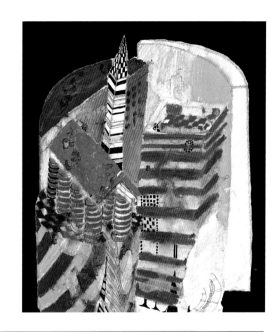

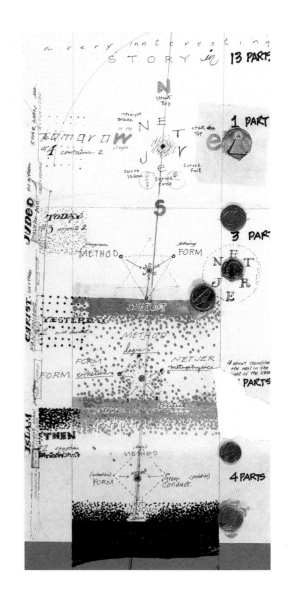

side of the beachfront location), filled with reference books and artifacts. Jerde's somber yet fanciful office is more John Soane than corporate titan. His design methods are more artist than businessman—even though he is an extremely savvy businessman. In wild paintings and drawings Jerde sketches the impression of a place, of a fantasy environment, of explosive energy fields. The Starbucks and Gaps come later.

The **boardwalk** might be a stimulus, but for Jerde the office is primarily a place for "interaction." The true source of peace and inspiration is his own home, the **Stone House**. It is in this picturesque, rustic house, buried in a canyon in the Santa Monica mountains, that Jerde does most of his creative work. Built over two decades (by a previous owner), the house is dark, eccentric, suffused with the odor of wood floors and paneling. It is quite unlike the festive environments Jerde creates, and much less high-tech. Materials are all natural, fireplaces are the only source of heat, and there isn't a computer in sight. In other ways, it reflects his work, with textured surfaces, decorative furnishing and a potpourri of art objects that are a testimony to his eclectic worldview. In a low-lit office with wood-paneled walls, or outside, at a table in his huge garden in the belly of the canyon, Jerde will work, often in collaboration with a designer, until, he says, "the design's popped." And then he goes to the office, "to watch things mature"[28] and "become manifest"[29] under the guidance of his fifteen project leaders. This primitive house embodies Jerde's paradoxical architectural goal: to imbue commercial, modern, high-tech environments with a sense of the organic, of having accreted over time.

Complexity and Contradiction

Given the many ideas and forces that Jerde's work is trying to harness, it is as fascinating for its many paradoxes as for its sheer scale and bravura. The Jerde Partnership sells itself as creator of architecture in which happenstance, accident and the firm's co-creative process generate seemingly organic environments. Yet its projects have a very distinct character. The exaggerated street life, the highly picturesque, narrative styling, evoke the locale in a way that is both intensified, even themed, and yet diluted with global flavors and transnational franchises.

The firm strives to create the patina of time, in a vast new district that may have to be built in under five years. The building types of the Jerde projects are the ones that tend to cut costs and use stage-set devices for visual effect, however, rather than the lovingly crafted and durable stone and brick environments of Jerde's ideals. He seeks a communal, democratic environment, yet most of his malls are privately owned and attract what he describes as a "community of consumers," brought into close proximity for a few hours, with no relationship or commitment to each other or the space. But this, he points out, is "just like ordinary cities."[30]

Despite this application of an artificial patina, Jerde's work represents the present and the future, a future that is not only postmodern but also post-GATT and NAFTA, a world of shifting international finance and shifting identities. In his essay, "And, Tomorrow … the World?," Craig Hodgetts describes how Jerde's "designs would, quite frankly, be unthinkable in a world without television, modems, global brands and the appetites they have created." And as Norman M. Klein explains in his essay, "The

Electronic Baroque," today's is a latter-day Baroque mercantile civilization, in which corporations have replaced popes and kings as clients, and for which **Jerde's exploding, illusory designs** are perhaps an appropriate expression.

The Language of Transformation

As part and parcel of the design and marketing process for his work Jon Jerde has invented a lexicon of words and phrases to articulate his concepts. "Armature" for example, is the main street or organizing spatial structure around which the elements in the project are arranged. The armature is effectively a corridor, or axis, or spine, drawing vistors through a linear but rarely straight sequential experience. There are many versions of this, such as the East and West wings and circular plaza at CityWalk; the double-curved diagonal slashing through six blocks at Horton Plaza; the below-level promenade at Beursplein; and the winding arcade in Bellagio. One of the most embedded terms is "placemaking," to describe the making of places rather than buildings. "Co-creative" is the design process involving teams of designers from different disciplines working together from the outset of a project, and sometimes also the development's tenants who are encouraged to add their own identity to the mix. "Experiential design" is the design of a movable experience, that picks up the thread of history and changes and evolves along a physical timeline.

For the purposes of understanding the kinds of urban transformations this book features, the architectural projects are divided into two groups, transformative and formative, relating to the two types of environments in which Jerde Partnership projects occur and their effects thereon.

Beach boardwalk, Santa Monica, California, USA.

The Stone House, Santa Monica, California, USA.

Original artwork by Jon Jerde, mixed media.

Transformative

Many of the firm's schemes are in built-up areas in inner cities and suburbs that have been blighted or fallen into decline or have no recognizable civic purpose. While to varying degrees self-contained, given that most are privately owned commercial centers, transformative projects have a physical connection with their surroundings, a connection that is reinforced through planning and architectural styling.

In the 1996 **Beursplein** project, the Jerde Partnership was asked to find a way to rescue Rotterdam's post-WWII shopping areas, severed by the city's busiest thoroughfare. The firm's solution was to sink the curving shopping street—the armature—under the highway, restoring access to and from major shopping districts. At Fashion Island, the Jerde Partnership breathed new life into this failing suburban mall in Newport Beach, California, by reshaping the space between the buildings. By introducing an urban scale to a suburban space, it was revived.

By roofing over a street, Jerde transformed another neighborhood, this time five blocks of downtown Las Vegas, reborn as **The Fremont Street Experience**. There, the solution was to transform the street into a pedestrian destination by roofing over the existing street with a 100 foot (30 m.) high space frame, and enticing an audience with an hourly nighttime "Light Spectacular."

Transformative projects can take the form of strategic maneuvres, as exemplified in the roofing and pedestrianization of Fremont Street or the condensing of Fashion Island. Or they can be newly built insertions into the city, as in Horton Plaza or One Reeperbahn. Another example, the Del Mar Plaza, is an upscale, gracious retail center and piazza on a corner site on the main street of a Southern Californian seaside town.

One of the largest insertions into the city fabric to date is **Canal City Hakata**. While clearly a self-contained destination, Canal City has, perhaps most importantly, sewn the seeds of urban renewal. It is connected to the adjacent districts by the canal, and, to get there, visitors must traverse declining neighborhoods. Merchants in nearby Kamikawabata were initially fearful of the project; they believed it would cause canal *gensho*, or "canal death," by drawing their last few customers away. Eventually they came to embrace it, even upgrading their own stores—efforts which paid off, with thousands of new passersby going to and from Canal City frequenting their businesses.

It must be noted, however, that these projects, in revitalizing one part of the city, may draw life from elsewhere, or displace existing businesses. While the livelihoods of the merchants of Kamikawabata, were revived by the arrival of Canal City Hakata, other major shopping districts in town have reportedly lost many of their customers to the new development. On the other hand, some of Jerde's projects are so distinctive and successful that they not only increase the land values in the surrounding district, but they become powerful attractions, increasing tourism and income for the city in general.

Indeed, the pulling power of these projects is such that historic cities, like Rotterdam, are hoping that the Jerde effect will rub off on them. LA-based Jerde, who draws his inspiration mainly from the dense urbanity of Europe, has now been hired by Europeans to help them restore their cities. The Jerde Partnership has been commissioned to design **One Reeperbahn** and transform the image of the St. Pauli red light district. In Warsaw, the firm intends its Zlota Center project to mend the fractured historic fabric of the city with clear axial planning and a public park.

In transformative projects the armature creates not only new streets but also connects to the grid of the surrounding neighborhood. The project exteriors are tailored with visual cues to evoke and capture the emotional resonance of the local cityscape, what Jerde calls "host place," without resorting to pastiche. They have a more distinctive character on the interior of the project, the destination.

Formative

The other setting for a Jerde project is on virgin territory, unbuilt land, both in and outside cities and suburbs. There, the challenge is to create from a blank slate a commercially viable, communal environment with a distinctive identity and a sense of stability. This is a paradoxical challenge given that cities are multilayered environments that have evolved over time and, furthermore, these fresh sites provide limited or even no architectural and environmental cues. These formative projects include **Bellagio**, an Italianate concoction on the Las Vegas Strip that joins a cacophony of themed casinos with no relationship to each other, all screaming for attention; the Universal City Masterplan, a platonic "city on a hill" inside a movie studio, and the micro-universe of Makuhari Town Center. These projects are relatively self-contained projects, each a world-within-a-world that forms a new and distinct identity for the locale.

One of the more notable and controversial of these formative projects is Mall of America, outside

Beursplein, Rotterdam, The Netherlands.

The Fremont Street Experience, Las Vegas, Nevada, USA.

Canal City Hakata, Fukuoka, Japan.

One Reeperbahn, Hamburg, Germany.

Bellagio, Las Vegas, Nevada, USA.

Bloomington, Minneapolis. Sprouted from virgin land near the local airport, Mall of America is a climate-controlled, micro-universe, with little connection to the flat, cold environment outside. There you can finish high school, go to college, get married, take the kids to Camp Snoopy, go to an aquarium, play golf, eat and go to movies—without ever leaving. So complete a destination is it that **Mall of America** attracts bus-, car- and plane-loads of tourists, many from Asia, who will spend several days at the mall without ever venturing out to see Minneapolis.

Urban Transformations

What all the Jerde projects have in common, however, at least in intention, is that they can be catalysts for urban development or renewal. Some of the Jerde Partnership's projects have successfully triggered new investment in their surroundings, even reinvigorated neighborhoods considered to be in irreversible decline, prompting the firm to append the marketing phrase "value added" to their projects. This lure of "value added," or exponential return, has made the Jerde Partnership the darling not just of developers but of city officials who, in a time of dwindling public resources, look to retail centers as revenue generators and engines of economic renewal. As far as Jerde himself is concerned, the added value is not only in maximizing a client and a city's return but also in creating a public space that offers something "for citizens, not consumers."

For over thirty years, Jerde has pursued his mission to create community—to restore urban vitality to cities and suburbs that had lost it through segregation of uses; to inject fantasy, variety and joy into architecture and planning

drained of such qualities by Modernism; to create place instead of space.

Jerde started with shopping centers. He once candidly observed that "the shopping center is a pretty pathetic venue to deal with broadbased communalizing, but it is all we've got and it's the pump-primer in America."[31] His firm's work has been attacked by critics in the architecture community and cultural élite who find distasteful the notion that shopping could be "the glue," despite the evidence of thousands of years of communal spaces whose primary function is the exchange of goods. But, having found a way to prime the pump in a way that satisfies clients and enables broadbased communalizing, Jerde is going on to realize his dream of creating multiuse districts in major cities around the world. He has proven that in a private world, public space can exist, that in a fractured society, community does want to form. He has persuaded cynical developers, chain stores, casino operators, city officials, home-builders, **movie theater** owners, restaurateurs and other designers that by harnessing their efforts, the civic realm can be revived. He has helped change the notion of who creates public space and in doing so, has created buildings that define our time—for that he demands our attention.

1   From "The Jerde Partnership, Reinventing the Communal Experience… A Problem Of Place," *Process: Architecture* No. 101, February 1992.

2   From Jon Jerde's writings in "Visceral Reality," *L'Arca Edizioni spa* 1998.

3   From an interview with Jon Jerde by the author, March 14, 1997.

4   From a conversation with the author, January 18, 1999.

5   Experiential design is more sophisticated than themed design. Themed environments evoke or re-create an image, place or idea, usually a fantasy—such as Arabian Nights or eighteenth-century theming. This can also be called narrative in that it tells a story. Experiential design is designed to a further level, which appeals to all the senses—smells and sounds are as considered as

the sights—while also involving the visitor in assimilating the information provided by their surroundings. CityWalk is not a themed re-creation of Los Angeles, for example, rather it suggests elements that people recognize, and builds an evocation of something familiar. At New York New York, the eponymous Las Vegas casino, in contrast, takes the most recognizable elements and miniaturizes them exactly.

6   Paul Goldberger, "Freewheeling Fantasy in San Diego," *The New York Times*, March 19, 1986.

7   David Wharton, "A Walk on the Mild Side," *Los Angeles Times*, May 27, 1994.

8   Ada Louise Huxtable, *The Unreal America: Architecture and Illusions*, (New York: The New Press, 1997), p. 10.

9   Ada Louise Huxtable, *op. cit.*, p. 58.

10   Jane Jacobs, *The Death and Life of Great American Cities*, (New York: Vin Books and Random House, 1961).

11   From the *LA Business Journal's* "1998 Lists."

12   From Jon Jerde's writings, January 10, 1997.

13   From a conversation with the author, January 18, 1999.

14   *Ibid.*

15   Charles Jencks, *Architecture of the Jumping Universe*, (London: Academy Editions, 1995), p. 130.

16   From Jon Jerde's writings, January 13, 1997.

17   *Ibid.*

18   *Ibid.*

19   John Brinckerhoff Jackson, *Discovering The Vernacular Landscape*, (New Haven, Connecticut: Yale University Press, 1984), p. 17.

20   John Brinckerhoff Jackson, *op. cit.*

21   From a conversation with the author, January 18, 1999.

22   From a conversation with the author, December 1998.

23   From Jon Jerde's writings, January 22, 1997.

24   Notes to the author, January 1999.

25   From an interview with Jon Jerde by the author, March 14, 1997.

26   Ada Louise Huxtable, *op. cit.*, p. 103.

27   From an interview with Jon Jerde by the author, January 18, 1999.

28   From an interview with Jon Jerde by the author, August 14, 1998.

29   Notes to the author, January 1999.

30   *Ibid.*

31   From an interview with Jon Jerde by the author, March 14, 1997.

Mall of America, Bloomington, Minnesota, USA.

Universal CityWalk, Universal City, California, USA.

Los Angeles Olympic Games In 1983 Jon Jerde headed the team of Los Angeles architects, graphic designers and artists who transformed 1,000 square miles of Los Angeles into a festive public arena for the 1984 Olympic Games. The team, using a "kit of parts" of inexpensive off-the-shelf materials, designed this colorful and imaginative event that was seen by millions of people around the world.

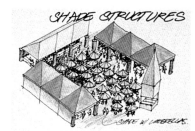
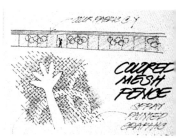

The 1984 Olympics was the first privately organized Games and the Los Angeles Olympic Organizing Committee was determined not only to set an example of fiscal restraint, but to make the event profitable. It spent roughly $500 million on the Games, seven percent of Moscow's expenditure in 1980. Of this, about $10 million (two percent) was earmarked for the style and "look" of the Games, from event programs to concessionaire accessories, tickets and judges' blazers to street decorations and highway signage, from field-of-play equipment, information booths, and stadiums to three athletes' villages.

This minimal budget precluded the erection of "heroic" structures; instead, the committee called for a no-frills approach using as many existing facilities as possible. Jon Jerde was initially invited to design the UCLA Olympic Village. Olympics CEO Peter Ueberroth's response to Jerde's conceptual design was so enthusiastic, however, that he appointed Jerde "design czar" and encouraged him to develop a more ambitious strategy for the Games.

The brief was to transform 75 Olympic sports and Arts Festival venues, ten freeway systems, thirty boulevards, twelve transportation centers and three Olympic villages within a 100-mile radius of downtown Los Angeles. The design needed to reflect the cultural diversity of Southern California and the international spirit of the Olympics. It was to be a signature for the Games that was bold, repetitive, reusable and flexible. And, while not monumental, it still needed to be cohesive, powerful and telegenic.

Together with the environmental graphic design firm Sussman/Prezja, the Jerde Partnership developed an architectural makeover in the form of a "kit of parts." Taking an assemblage of catalogued, archetypal pieces, some thirty design teams, using simple rules of operation under Jerde's supervision, transformed each of the Olympic sites.

The kit of parts appropriated low-cost materials as components: rentable scaffolding, cheap fabric normally used to cover buildings during construction, cardboard tubes used to form concrete, fiberglass produce trays, machines that put striping on city streets, rented party

From above, clockwise: Notes and drawings that detailed the kit of parts—an assemblage of archetypal elements—given to the thirty design teams.

Below left: A page from the "kit of parts" booklet distributed to the design teams.

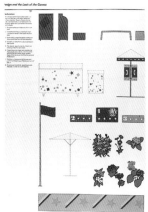

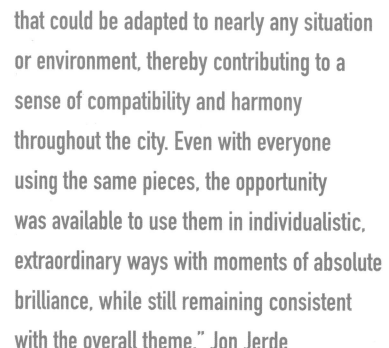

"The kit of parts was a catalogue of pieces that could be adapted to nearly any situation or environment, thereby contributing to a sense of compatibility and harmony throughout the city. Even with everyone using the same pieces, the opportunity was available to use them in individualistic, extraordinary ways with moments of absolute brilliance, while still remaining consistent with the overall theme." Jon Jerde

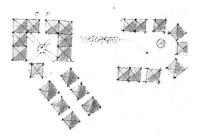

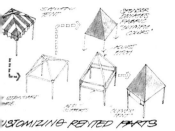

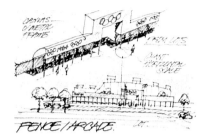

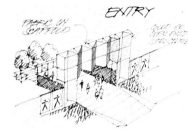

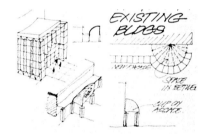

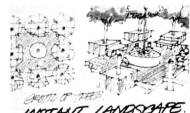

tents. Using what Jerde calls an "architecture of economy," the teams devised simple yet dramatic strategies to link events across the metropolis, with a theme of lightweight structures, giant canvas shapes, signage, tenting, banners and fabric-wrapped palm trees. All was rendered in a palette of vivid colors (magenta, aqua, vermilion, chrome yellow). For the first time, a design for the Games expressed the momentary rather than the permanent. A temporary identity for the Los Angeles Olympics was formed from folded paper and confetti instead of poured-in-place concrete and etched stone.

During the 1984 Olympic Games visitors and citizens saw the city in a coherent state for the first time, as did millions of television viewers around the world. Before the Games, some Angelenos scoffed; others left town; some

detractors, citing past Games, argued the project would be a huge waste of money. Instead, the Games exceeded even the optimists' wildest expectations. It was such a success that it has become a model for subsequent Olympics.

Three of the ideas that the Jerde Partnership has continued to utilize evolved with this project: the kit of parts or notion of creating projects out of interchangeable, off-the-shelf elements; the firm's concept of co-creativity, in which multidisciplinary design teams collaborate from the inception on a project to give it a pluralistic rather than singular voice; and its conviction that large-scale, temporary urban transformations can be designed.

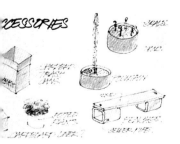

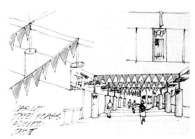

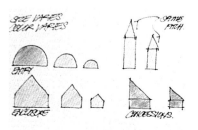

This page and following pages:
Graphic elements, using a palette
of vivid colors created by Deborah
Sussman of Sussman/Prejza, characterized each of the 75 venues.

Horton Plaza is a 1.5 million square foot, six-block profusion of shops, restaurants, movie theaters and public space in downtown San Diego that challenged conventional suburban mall planning and helped trigger economic revitalization in a blighted city center. At Horton Plaza, completed in 1985, the Jerde Partnership developed the notion of the armature, or winding spine, where the spaces between the buildings are as important as the buildings themselves.

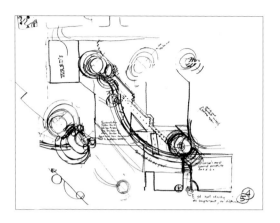

YOU ARE HERE ↓

In 1977 the legendary developer Ernest Hahn proposed to build a shopping center on 11.5 acres (4.6 ha.) in downtown San Diego, one of America's ailing urban centers. Sensing that something extraordinary was necessary to lure people back from suburban mega-malls, Hahn contacted Jerde. As head of design at the retail architecture firm Charles Kober Associates, Jerde had spent over a decade formulating his theory about shopping malls: the retail industry focused on function and rationality. The standard, market-formulated shopping centers that had proliferated across the USA in the 1970s were, in Jerde's opinion, outdated. Designed as machines for shopping, pure and simple, malls lacked, he believed, the kind of complex experience found in existing urban conditions. Shopping is a communal act. Rather than denigrate malls as vacuous, anti-urban conditions, he argued, recognize them as de facto meeting points, places of spontaneous experience for citizens living and working in endless suburban sprawl. The shopping center could provide, if brought back into the city, a setting that acted as a catalyst to renew a public life of richness and complexity. In his vision, the design focus is on the user. "Design shopping centers for citizens," he said, "not consumers."

Jerde's ideas had met with resistance until Hahn approached him to design Horton Plaza. When Jerde accepted the commission it made it possible for him to set up his own office, The Jerde Partnership International. He and his team set to work remaking the shopping mall prototype, breaking many of the rules of shopping center design in the process.

Traditional malls feature a "dumbbell" plan; department stores anchor each end of a long, straight concourse in which shoppers can see from one end to the other. At Horton Plaza, Jerde "wanted to create an irresistible place." He traded the rational, linear organization for the picturesque, creating a multilevel, double-curved diagonal "street," an armature that links four department-store anchors. This street acts as an axis that connects the downtown area to the waterfront. Alternately narrow and wide, covered and open, the street's four staggered levels include balconies, nooks, towers, bridges—people-watching spaces that transform shopping into *passegiata*.

The armature at Horton Plaza refers to a variety of vernacular urban models—the Italian hill town, Venice, the Arab casbah—built around social patterns and topographic conditions. Horton Plaza, with its lighthearted colorful buildings (peach, mauve, terracotta), creates the illusion of a street, a refracted, exaggerated, stick-and-

Above: Sketch plan of internal street: multilevel, double-curved diagonal links four department stores.

Opposite: Jon Jerde's sketches show how the project is composed of fragments of indigenous architecture.

"Retail centers are created for everybody: they speak in the language of the populace. But I knew they would be better designed for citizens, not just consumers." Jon Jerde

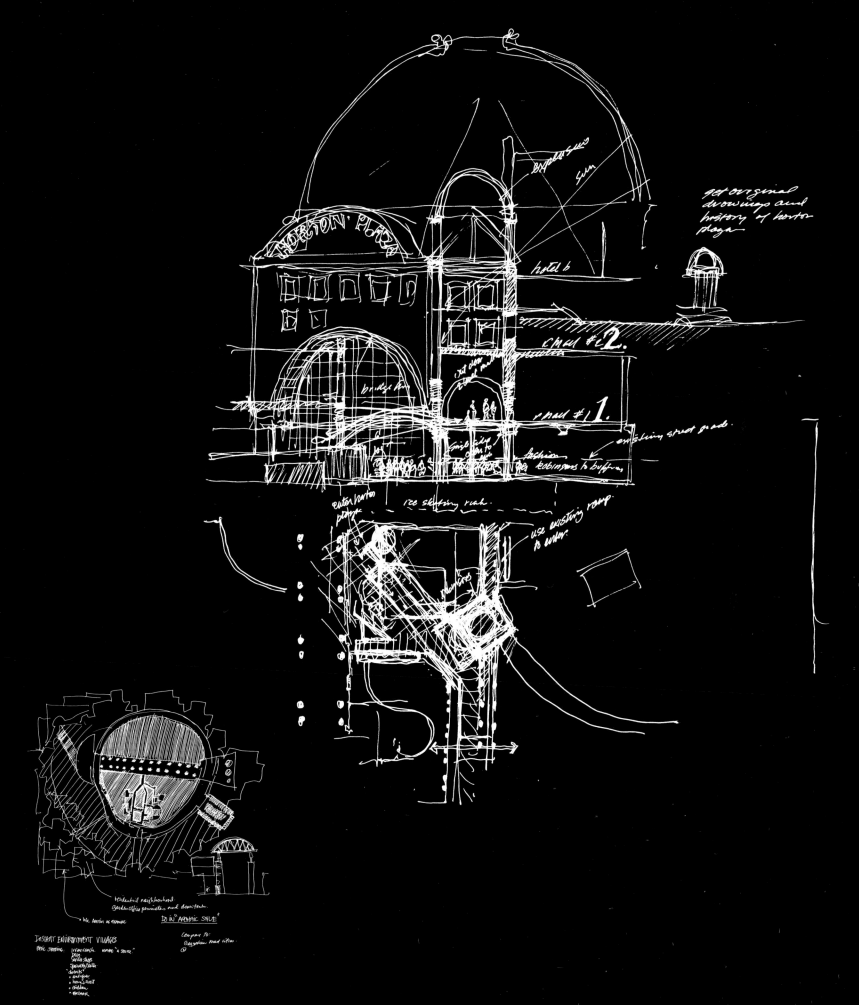

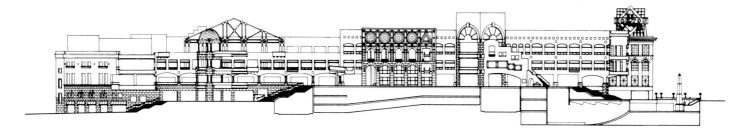

Above: Longitudinal section.

stucco stage-set for public activities. "Horton Plaza should not be thought of as a building, but rather as a zone or place within the urban center of San Diego, where anyone can be assured of the conviviality of throngs of people walking its streets, plazas, bridges and terraces from early morning to late at night," Jerde wrote as he began to plan the project.

Horton Plaza is a suburban building-type introduced into an urban setting. It is knitted into the city's existent grid pattern, the armature connects nearby streets, and its architectural aesthetic, composed around fragments of existing buildings, reflects San Diego's rich architectural history. The strolling arcades are defined by deep set arches, mosaics and tile domes. Signage, fountains, anonymous artifacts, canopies, sculpture and art are added, making Horton Plaza a complex, multilayered urban environment.

Horton Plaza has weathered and become embedded into the psyche of San Diego. The intention was that it should convey the sense of always having been there, having been designed not by a single hand, but by many, thus embodying the pluralism of intact urban environments. To achieve this, Jerde tailored the design process, organizing the project into six separate components: the anchor department stores, the long galleria building, the transportation building, the southernmost court, the sports terrace, and the marketplace. Co-creative teams of designers, each working on an element independently, offered a spontaneous reaction and individual solutions.

The project, built in eighteen months, with a minimal budget of $140 million, opened with the expectation that it would take five years to become profitable. Instead, it was instantly successful. In its first year, 25 million people visited the project. Since its opening, Horton Plaza has inspired acres of private- and city-sponsored housing, new office buildings, a convention center, light rail transportation and waterfront development. The project has increased the city's revenues and investments, and transformed it into an active civic center and international destination.

Today, Jerde comments that "Horton was crude, but it was a great beginning. We had no real models, not only for the building type, but for the appropriate design process itself." This challenges most traditional architectural and urban design thinking—particularly Modernist architecture that strives to create memorably individual buildings—by focusing on the spaces in-between and the user's experience of "place."

Opposite: Aerial view of Horton Plaza under construction.

Below: Axonometric drawing of Horton Plaza and surrounding buildings. Horton became a catalyst for revitalization in other parts of the city.

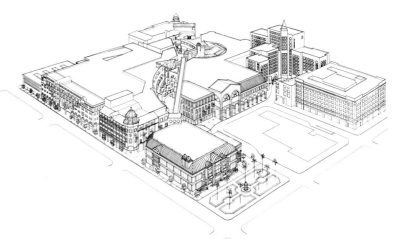

Horton Plaza, San Diego, California, USA

Below: Entrance to
Horton Plaza.

Opposite, from left: Views of
internal street, multilevel
terraced promenade and bridges
connecting both sides.

Opposite: Horton Plaza was not intended to be a collection of buildings; its individual elements contribute to making it a unique six-block district of the city.

This page: Signage, fountains, artifacts, canopies, sculpture and art were easily layered against the fragments of San Diego's architecture. Horton's rich colors were influenced by the warm climate of Southern California.

The Architect and the Mall Margaret Crawford

Mention Jon Jerde's name in architectural circles and an argument is sure to start. Jerde sees himself as an urban visionary, a humanist who can produce "community" and "experiential places" on demand. Urban critics, on the other hand, have portrayed him as dangerous to the "real" city, a huckster marketing simulation and shopping as genuine urban experience.[1] Architecturally, Jerde considers himself a renegade, more concerned with evolving ideas than with architectural style while many architects think his work borders on kitsch. But to anyone interested in the evolution of the shopping mall, Jerde's status is unquestionable: he is a towering figure, one of only two architects—the other was Victor Gruen, the inventor of the enclosed shopping mall—who have been able to shape the form of this fundamental late twentieth-century building type.

Gruen and Jerde stand out in a field that celebrates the developers who generate the malls, rather than the architects who design them. Gruen's innovations defined the form and formula of the archetypal Modernist mall—**the indoor regional shopping mall**—that spread across the United States in the years from 1960 to 1980. Operating in a climate that demands more rapid changes in form and product, Jerde, has produced, in typically postmodern fashion, a succession of different mall types. However, Gruen and Jerde's consistent success at mall design is based on the same paradoxical talent; their ability to simultaneously satisfy a set of seemingly contradictory requirements. First, and fundamentally, they must adhere to the rigid formulas that govern a mall's profitability. At the same time, however, they need to generate continual innovation, in order to stay at the forefront of the constantly changing state-of-the-art mall. These are minimal requirements; what has made Gruen and Jerde legendary was the addition of yet a third element to the mall: a communicable mood of sociability. Tapping into popular desires and their own cravings for urbanity, they learned how to orchestrate communal pleasure.

Gruen and Jerde were not the first architects to successfully operate at the juncture of such conceptually disparate architectural practices. Raymond Hood, William van Alen and **John Portman**, to mention three, occupied similar territory. And, like Gruen and Jerde, their work has always presented problems for critics and historians. Too popular to be acceptable as high art yet too formally adept to dismiss, they occupy a liminal space between conventional critical categories. Premature practitioners of the postmodern philosophy of "both/and," their work collapses a series of linked polarities: between the commercial and the artistic, the popular and the pure, and, of course, the high and the low.

The Art and Science of Malling

Jerde did not start out to become a master of shopping mall design. After graduating from the University of Southern California's School of Architecture in 1964, he set up his own small practice, like many young architects with artistic aspirations, accepting the trade-off between artistic independence and financial rewards. Several years later, a financial crisis forced him to accept a job as design director for Charles Kober Associates, a large commercial firm specializing in the burgeoning field of shopping mall design. By the late 1960s, developers and designers had honed standard real-estate, financing, marketing and design techniques to create a predictable—and highly profitable—formula for the regional mall. Drawing customers from a 20-mile radius, containing at least two department stores and a hundred smaller stores, and organized around an enclosed atrium space, the standardized regional mall had become a necessity of suburban life.

In the rapidly growing Southern California region, the process that one writer called "The Malling of America" was almost complete.[2] Jerde and his staff produced standardized malls to plug the few remaining holes in Southern California's nearly saturated landscape of malls. Northridge Mall (1971), Hawthorne Plaza (1977), Glendale Galleria (1976) and Los Cerritos Plaza (1971) were all updated versions of the standard dumbbell mall, located in LA suburbs. Jerde provided just enough architecture to enliven the long corridors lined with chain stores and to distract shoppers from the sameness of predesigned department stores. Design had become as rule-driven as the highly structured system of mall development and financing, created to minimize guesswork. The architect was only one member of a team of experts that also included real-estate brokers, financial and marketing analysts, economists, merchandising experts, engineers, transportation planners and interior designers. Drawing on the latest academic and commercial methodologies, their goal was to guarantee the maximum dollar-per-square-foot yield. During the "golden" years of mall development, from 1950 to 1970, this approach was nearly foolproof; **malls spread out across the American landscape**, profits soared, and fewer than one percent of malls failed. As Edward DeBartolo, one of the country's largest developers, exulted, a shopping mall was "the best investment known to man."

Victor Gruen, Northland Mall, Detroit, Michigan, USA.
Victor Gruen, Eaton's Mall, Vancouver, Canada.

John Portman, Bonaventure Hotel, Los Angeles, California, USA.

Zeidler Roberts, Sherway Gardens Mall, Toronto, Canada.
Cesar Pelli & Associates, Simpson Court, Toronto, Canada.

Like most mall designers, Jerde had little creative freedom. Insisting on predictability, developers forced architects to stick to existing formulas. The system operated much like television programming, with each network presenting slightly different configurations of the same elements. Apparent diversity masked fundamental homogeneity. The last major design innovation had occurred in 1956, when Gruen designed the first enclosed mall, Southdale, outside of Minneapolis, Minnesota. Gruen's breakthrough had been motivated less by the desire for newness than to address two practical problems. The first, created by the ever-increasing size of malls, was the horizontal sprawl of the single-level outdoor shopping center. The second was the weather in Minnesota, which allowed only 126 outdoor shopping days a year. Gruen brilliantly solved both problems by enclosing two levels of shopping floors around a central court, providing a compact and focused circulation pattern. Enclosed open space and controlled temperatures produced a newly introverted type of building, with minimal perceptual connections with its surroundings.

This produced two contrary effects. The first was "retail drama." The newly enclosed indoor atrium provided a focused space for architects to manipulate and intensify. Southdale's atrium centerpiece, "the Garden Court of Perpetual Spring," filled with orchids, azaleas and palms, merely exaggerated the differences between the freezing cold or blistering heat outdoors with the mall's constant 72-degree Fahrenheit temperature. Subsequent atrium designs became increasingly extravagant, with spectacular spaces soaring vertically, offsetting the horizontal monotony of repetitious shopfronts. Skylights, landscaping and banks of zig-zagging escalators created even more exotic effects. These spaces, far more compelling than anything else in suburbia, popularized enclosed malls even in the mildest climates. Newly consolidated space also altered the commercial identity of the mall. Originally built to provide convenient one-stop suburban shopping, the glamorized malls now replaced the stores that served daily needs—supermarkets, hardware stores and drugstores—with specialty shops and fast-food arcades. Sealed off from the tasks of everyday life, shopping became a recreational activity.

Another effect of focusing so intensively on the interior was to turn the exterior of the mall into a windowless fortress, punctuated by minimal entrances. Since malls required only internal coherence, their exterior shells became a type of nonarchitecture. The need for continuous remodeling and expansion, and contracts allowing department stores to provide their own standardized buildings, exacerbated the situation. As a result, from a distance most malls looked like ungainly piles of oversized boxes plunked down in the middle of an asphalt sea. Without an immediate urban context, surrounded by landscaping, acres of parking and roads, each mall became a separate enclave. This followed a typical suburban pattern: an atomized landscape of pedestrian islands, completely disconnected from one another. Without sidewalks, malls were accessible only by automobiles. In this environment of access roads, off ramps and parking spaces, traditional design elements such as scale, facades, and detailing became irrelevant.

By 1968, when Jerde designed his first mall, the architectural possibilities of the enclosed mall had reached their limits. Gruen's innovative solution had turned into conventional wisdom. Standardized development and merchandising structured the organization of the mall, leaving only the atrium to the architect. Modernism, still imprisoned by its commitment to abstraction, standardization, and technology, provided additional constraints. This limited architectural efforts to elaborate and differentiate these fundamentally generic spaces to two options. The first was to aggrandize the monumental qualities of interior space using dramatic but clearly articulated structural technology. In the **Fox Hills Mall** in Culver City, California, designed in 1976, Cesar Pelli expanded the atrium into the mall, creating an enormous unified volume flooded with natural light from a series of undulating scooped skylights.[3] Other designers followed the lead of Atlanta architect and developer John Portman, creating self-consciously artificial environments. This strategy defamiliarized atrium space by choreographing confusingly layered spaces and enlivening them with special effects such as plunging elevators, hanging gardens and water features. Disorientation enhanced otherwise banal experiences.

Crisis and Recovery

After a decade of designing malls, Jerde was convinced that there were other options. An executive vice president at Kober, he was bored and dissatisfied with the "cookie-cutter" malls he was turning out. Fluent in the language of retailing and development, he urged the firm's biggest client, Ernest Hahn, a developer based in San Diego, to build something new and different.[4] Jerde's instincts were right on the mark; both architectural tastes and the consumer markets were changing. After

Cesar Pelli & Associates, Fox Hills Mall, Culver City, California, USA.

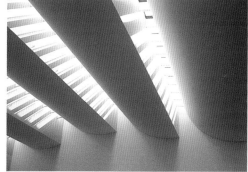

1970, it became evident that the postwar economic system of mass production and mass consumption that underlay the regional mall paradigm was breaking down. Employment, income and spending patterns were fragmenting into a much more complex mosaic. More flexible types of production appeared, emphasizing rapid cycles of products that quickly responded to the consumer markets' constantly changing needs and tastes. This picture was further complicated by an increasingly uneven geographic distribution of economic development, producing exaggerated differences between zones of prosperity and poverty. Competition heightened—between corporations, developers and even urban regions.

In this unstable situation, the continued development of existing mall types was no longer assured. Although the system of regional malls continued to flourish, it was clear that the generic mixes, merchandising and design no longer guaranteed profits. More specialized mall types began to appear, focused on specific market niches and lifestyles. The success of San Francisco's **Ghirardelli Square** (1964) and The Cannery (1968), tastefully renovated factories in spectacular urban locations, suggested alternatives to the contrived packaging, obvious manipulation and mass-market imagery of formula malls. This led developer James Rouse to develop a new mall type, the festival marketplace, rejecting the architectural homogeneity of the generic mall in favor of the unique character of an "authentic" single location enhanced by "individualized" design. Like Jerde, Rouse had a difficult time persuading financiers, retailers and city officials that renovating the Quincy Market and **Faneuil Hall** in Boston (1976) was a plausible concept, but its rapid and astonishing success led to a succession of festival marketplaces in scenic spots across the country.

At the same time, developers reinvented the suburban mall to fit into downtowns. Architects compressed sprawling malls to fit tight urban sites, making them more compact and vertical and attaching stacked floors of indoor parking. Supported by city governments searching for ways to revitalize downtowns, they received tax breaks and subsidies. In large, dense cities such as Chicago or New York, megastructure malls added traditional urban functions such as hotels, offices and apartments. Plaza Pasadena, Jon Jerde's last project with Kober and Hahn, was a modest effort to update Colorado Boulevard, Pasadena's fading main street. A joint venture with the city of Pasadena, the project was subject to numerous design reviews by local planners and citizens. Critics gave Jerde's attempts at contextual sensitivity—streetside shopfronts and an abstracted arch maintaining the axis of the Beaux-Arts civic center—guarded praise. Acknowledging that this was the best that could be done in the real world of cities and developers, they pointed out the limits of his victory. Jerde altered the look but not the form of the inward-facing mall.[5]

Crossover Dreams

However, these gestures were tentative compared with the dramatic changes taking place in architectural culture. Responding to the challenges to the Modernist credo put forth in the late 1960s by Robert Venturi, Jane Jacobs and others, architects had already begun to explore the richness of historical and urban contexts. The open, inclusive and eclectic spirit of early postmodernism, although it lasted less than a decade, expanded the boundaries of architecture. Looking across time and space, architects embraced ornament and color as well as historical and localized allusions. A newly populist point of view acknowledged the importance of mass taste and of creating places that responded to human needs.

In Los Angeles, Charles Moore personified these values. In spite of his years as Dean of Yale's architectural school, Moore gave them a particularly Californian spin. His 1965 article, "You Have to Pay for the Public Life," signaled a new attitude towards public space, a topic largely ignored by Modernist architectural discourse. Moore identified popular California tourist venues such as the Nut Tree (a roadside restaurant near Sacramento) and Disneyland as uniquely pleasurable public places. He celebrated Disneyland's make-believe qualities, pointing out that it was one of the few places where Southern Californians could experience traditional, if scaled down, urban space.

Moore's openness was legendary. A list of his favorite places and buildings was dizzying; including Beverly Hills, the garden of Bomarzo, the Brighton Pavilion, Hadrian's Villa, mansard-roofed trailers, Texas breweries and Cape Cod barns.[6] His design for the **Piazza d'Italia** in New Orleans, Louisiana (1975), pushed eclecticism to a new extreme. A scenographic collage commissioned by the city's Italian community, the project mixed high art allusions to the Trevi fountain and **Palladio's Basilica in Vicenza** with popular idioms such as neon and brightly painted surfaces, camp motifs such as the Delicatessen Order (based on sausages) and a fountain shaped like Italy.

In this permissive climate, Jerde cast off the last vestiges of Modernism. Jerde knew Moore well and the two had even discussed collaborating.

Lawrence Halprin & Associates, Ghirardelli Square, San Francisco, California, USA.

Benjamin Thompson Associates, Faneuil Hall and Quincy Market, Boston, Massachusetts, USA.

Charles Moore, Piazza d'Italia, New Orleans, Louisiana, USA.

Andrea Palladio, Basilica, Vicenza, Italy.

Jerde's own European experiences, beginning after college with a year-long Architectural Guild Traveling Fellowship, had already developed his appreciation of complex and small-scale urban spaces. Moreover, unlike Moore, whose temperament and dedication to academic life limited his practice to houses and small institutional projects, Jerde had the contacts and the expertise to directly apply his ideas to large-scale commercial projects. His most significant opportunity came in 1977, when Ernest Hahn approached him with an enormous mall project, **Horton Plaza**, to be located in the center of San Diego's decaying downtown. On the promise of this single commission Jerde opened his own office and began work. The development of Horton Plaza was a complex drawn-out process—it opened only in 1985—which began as a standard regional mall. The final design still contained the familiar contents of an urban regional mall—four department stores, 150 shops, a hotel, movie theaters, and a parking structure with 2,400 parking spaces—but its form was radically new.

Paradoxically, Horton Plaza both resisted and incorporated mall formulas; while undeniably innovative, it also drew upon the successful elements of regional malls and festival marketplaces. Intended to attract tourists to downtown San Diego, it was not enclosed, making the most of San Diego's benign climate and downtown sea breezes. Avoiding Rouse's tasteful quaintness, Jerde opted for a fully fledged commercial postmodernism. Explicitly theatrical, it took retail drama to a new level of fantasy and exuberance. A complex assemblage of architectural elements organized along a diagonal circulation spine that sliced through the six-block site, Horton Plaza was the antithesis of the orthogonal legibility of most malls. Jerde orchestrated a variety of distinctive spatial events based on the concept of a series of overlapping villages.

Beginning with the dramatic entry stairs ascending above street level, the many steps, bridges and ramps produce unexpected changes in level, reminiscent of those in an Italian hill town. Space expands and contracts as one moves through a narrow multileveled galleria that opens out to two expansive arced piazzas. A series of pavilion-like architectural elements—palazzo, tower and cathedral—protrude and overlap into these spaces, creating twists and turns, nooks and crannies. At different levels, thin screen walls with punched out openings further complicate the space, offering multiple vantage points.

Even more shocking, after decades of blankly abstract malls, Horton Plaza was a riot of color and patterned surfaces, some specifically mimicking historical forms, others making more abstract allusions. Two separate systems, one composed of overscaled historical elements—"supergraphics," in the parlance of the period—the other a vivid color palette, created by graphic designer Deborah Sussman, covered every available surface. Sussman, one of Jerde's main collaborators on the **Los Angeles Olympic Games**, derived 49 colors, including ochre, mauve and peach, from the San Diego environment, then applied them in various tones. Banners, vendor carts, street entertainers and kiosks further enlivened the spaces. Overall, the effect was festive, making a special event out of what was in truth a standard shopping experience.

Although Jerde claimed to be primarily inspired by his memories of specific urban places— the "intelligent geography of European cities," he says—he also clearly drew on the work of his postmodern contemporaries. Charles Moore's influence is most visible. Horton Plaza's visual and spatial complexity depends on many of Moore's innovations; screens that layer space, Mannerist and Baroque geometries such as diagonals, ovals and spirals, contrasts of scale, love of complexity, and above all, a visible interest in pleasure and wit. Other elements, such as the open gallery that cuts through the project, recall Aldo Rossi's De Chirico-like blind arcades. Still others suggest the pastel patterning of Michael Graves. Yet in spite of this virtuoso display of exuberant eclecticism inside the mall, Jerde did not overcome the problems inherent in the mall form. Horton Plaza remains inwardly focused, its peripheral parking garages and windowless department stores re-creating the fortresslike quality of the suburban mall.

Still, **Horton Plaza** was a popular and financial success. Although the mall's role in the revitalization of downtown San Diego is often exaggerated, it did rejuvenate downtown retail, attracting both tourists and residents. Its success also marked a definitive break in the evolution of the shopping mall, signaling the introduction of "theming" as an increasingly necessary element of mall design. Imagery began to play a key role in invigorating tired formulas. This pushed a basic marketing principle, "adjacent attraction," to a new extreme. Adjacent attraction is a form of indirect commodification where "the most similar objects lend each other mutual support when they are placed next to each other."[7] Increasingly, malls juxtaposed shopping with a spectacle of images and themes designed to communicate, entertain and stimulate.

Jerde called Horton Plaza an urban theme park, but it differs considerably from later fantasy-based malls. Although, as in a theme park, Jerde condensed and juxtaposed images of urbanity from

Catalog of kit of parts showing color palette, Los Angeles Olympic Games, Los Angeles, California, USA.

Horton Plaza, San Diego, California, USA.

Los Angeles Olympic Games, Los Angeles, California, USA.

Jon Jerde, sketches of Horton Plaza, San Diego, California, USA.

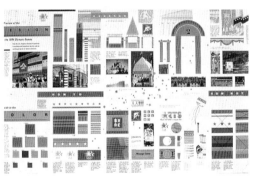

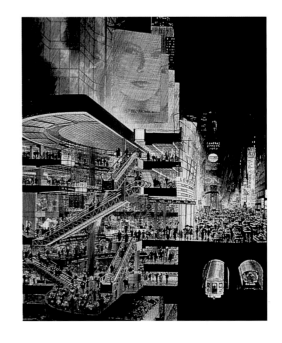

across time and space, he drew on a selective repertoire of urban and architectural images specifically relevant to the mall's function as a public space. In contrast to these highly focused and self-consciously postmodern borrowings, subsequent malls relied more on the Disneyland model, spatially compressing wildly disparate themes. This pattern of indiscriminate borrowing reached its peak at the West Edmonton Mall in Alberta, Canada. Here, a frenzy of images including a lagoon with real submarines, a dolphin arena, replicas of a Parisian stereoscope and New Orleans' Bourbon Street compete for the visitors' attention. Unlike these literal, if partial, representations, Horton Plaza's palazzos, cathedrals and bridges remain abstract distillations of their sources. Their scale and literal superficiality proclaim and emphasize their semiotic roles. Jerde called Horton Plaza "a great experiment—the first of its kind" but it has remained the only one of its kind. Its decorative surfaces opened the door for more explicit theming.

Surprisingly, the mall that is closest to Horton Plaza in intention and form is **Santa Monica Place**, designed in 1980 by Frank Gehry. Critics often portray Gehry as the high-art antithesis of Jerde's commercial populism; Rem Koolhaas called Jerde Gehry's evil twin.[8] But the two architects share many concerns. Like Jerde, Gehry had an extensive background in retail and commercial architecture. After graduating from USC, he worked for Victor Gruen Associates on mall projects for many years.[9] Santa Monica Place was very similar to Horton Plaza in many respects; both were set into the urban fabric (although Santa Monica Place is smaller—occupying only two city blocks) in scenic locations. Like Jerde, Gehry attempted to complexify spatial experience by purely architectural

means. Both malls are organized around diagonal axes with offset spaces (a food court and atrium at Santa Monica Place) that create unexpected angles and vistas. Both utilize a profusion of bridges, terraces and screenlike elements with punctured openings to further complicate the space. Gehry dramatized the tension between the complex interior diagram and the external street grid by pushing the internal structure through the exterior walls, creating a characteristic assemblage of colliding forms. Since the developer insisted on enclosure, Gehry connected the mall to its setting with a series of open terraces facing the ocean.

However, there were two crucial differences between the malls. First, in contrast to **Horton Plaza's** crowd-pleasing riot of colors and surfaces, Santa Monica Place remained resolutely abstract, a composition of white planar surfaces. This choice, surprising in an architect known for exploiting the distinctive texture of commonplace materials, visibly proclaimed an allegiance to high-art abstraction. Modernist purity legitimized the commercialism of the mall typology by linking it with the tradition of "white" architecture that stretched from Le Corbusier to Richard Meier. This contributed in part to the second difference between Horton Plaza and Santa Monica Place: Gehry's design was far less successful commercially. Less than ten years after it was built, the Rouse Company redesigned the mall's facades and interior for a less "generic" look. Color, graphics and other decorative elements, including fountains and palm trees, were added to convey a more specific sense of local character. At the same time, eliminating the terraces, providing even lighting, and other subtle changes improved the mall's effectiveness as a focused shopping environment.[10]

The World as a Mall

As much as critics have tried to assign Jerde a definitive role, his subsequent projects did not fit easily into even the categories he created himself. **Westside Pavilion**, a remodeling of a 1950s shopping center in West Los Angeles, completed in 1985, took on the problem of the blank exterior. To fit an enormous mall into a neighborhood of single-story houses and small commercial buildings, Jerde, again working with Deborah Sussman, used patterning to break down the mall's windowless street frontage into four pavilions, then subdivided each one into three-story facades, with restaurants and shops on the ground floor. As at Plaza Pasadena, the price for producing this lively streetscape was complete disjuncture between interior and exterior, without any visual or physical link between the arcaded interior and the street facades. The Jerde Partnership office took on every type of mall, from the low-key, woodsy **Village at Corte Madera** on the bayfront in Marin County, California to Mall of America, in Minneapolis, a mega-mall so large and inclusive it functions as a tourist destination. Redesigning and updating older malls (including those designed by Jerde for Kober) provided the Jerde Partnership with bread-and-butter work.

Jerde became one of the first designers to jump into a new mall genre—the entertainment mall. Jerde saw this more flexible form, whose rules had not yet been established, as a venue for experimentation. His approach, while still omnivorously eclectic, became less historicist. In 1989, he designed **Metropolis Times Square** for the center of Manhattan, a high-tech extravaganza that radically departed from his previous work. Never built, this six-level atrium space, inserted in a Skidmore,

Westside Pavilion, Los Angeles, California, USA.

Village at Corte Madera, Corte Madera, California, USA.

Frank O. Gehry & Associates, Santa Monica Place, Santa Monica, California, USA.

Horton Plaza, San Diego, California, USA.

Metropolis Times Square, New York, New York, USA.

Owings & Merrill skyscraper, was to be surrounded by a transparent electronic wall, the Whiz Bang, a programmable sign, sound, light and video system of 350 television sets. Operated by a video-jockey orchestrating audience input, the system would produce information, lighting and entertainment. In 1993 **Universal CityWalk** opened in Los Angeles. Created to connect massive parking garages with Universal City's two profitable anchors, a multiplex movie theater and the Universal Studios Theme Park, the project contains restaurants, entertainment venues and recreational shopping. CityWalk extends many of Horton Plaza's formal preoccupations, using an expanded vocabulary of bricolage materials, now including Modernist and high-tech elements. Facades that are organized around a shallow-domed space frame distill and exaggerate elements of Los Angeles' architectural past. They are juxtaposed with familiar mall forms, giant neon signs, and improbable landscaping to create a dreamlike space with undeniable intensity. The saturated market and recession of the early 1990s in Southern California presented few opportunities for further development in the home market. But the rapid boom and massive expansion of investment and consumption in the Pacific Rim made Asia the hot spot for all kinds of mall development. In Japan, **Canal City Hakata**, Jerde's newest and most innovative project, pushes eclecticism even further, piling on references from so many and such disparate sources that they become indecipherable.

Jerde's reputation has been shaped as much by the changes in the critical context as by his own development. In many respects, his formal and social concerns have remained consistent, while architectural values have shifted dramatically. Architectural critics, still under the spell of post-

modernism in the late 1980s, praised Horton Plaza. But by the time CityWalk appeared, only five years later, the critical climate had changed. Populism had disappeared from the architectural discourse, replaced by a neo-avant-garde position that, following the line of Frankfurt School critic Theodore Adorno,[11] saw any connection with consumerism or mass culture as dangerously complicit with capitalism and detrimental to the survival of architecture as an autonomous art.[12] Urban critics, borrowing from the work of theorists such as Guy Debord and Jean Baudrillard, attacked Jerde's mall imagery and created collectivity as part of a larger culture of spectacle and simulation that had replaced "real" social relations and "authentic" public spaces.[13]

In the face of this nearly universal critical condemnation, Jerde remains a thorn in the side of conventional architecture and easy distinctions between high and low. His prolific production and financial success—the Jerde Partnership is one of very few noncorporate firms that have achieved truly global practice—does not endear him to architects who posit an inevitable contradiction between architectural quality and monetary rewards. On the margins of an architectural discourse that privileges theoretical understanding, Jerde is notably unsuccessful. Even his own attempts to codify the principles behind his work are unconvincing: a mixture of leftover postmodern rhetoric, marketing slogans and autobiographical insights. It is more likely that Jerde operates without theoretical angst. Having, after so many years, internalized the demands of the marketplace, it has given him the freedom to be creative. An intuitive designer, he has managed to stay emotionally in touch with the preferences of large

numbers of people around the world. And, as a result, he is, probably more than any other living designer, transforming that world.

1   Ada Louise Huxtable, "Living with the Fake and Liking It," *The New York Times*, March 30, 1997.

2   William Kowinski, *The Malling of America* (New York: William Morrow, 1985).

3   The introduction of natural light into malls after 1973 was closely related to the dramatic rise in energy costs. Before this, 70 percent of energy use in malls was consumed by artificial lighting. See Barry Maitland, *Shopping Malls Planning and Design* (Harlow: Longman Scientific and Technical, 1985), p. 38n.

4   John Davidson, "Prophet of the Mall," *Buzz*, July/August 1992, pp. 69–73, 94.

5   John Morris Dixon, "Procession in Pasadena," *Progressive Architecture*, July 1981, pp. 94–97.

6   David Littlejohn, *Architect: the Life and Work of Charles W. Moore* (New York: Holt, Reinhardt and Winston, 1984), p. 156.

7   Richard Sennett, *The Fall of Public Man* (New York: Vintage, 1976), pp. 144–45.

8   From a lecture by Rem Koolhaas, "The Metropolis and Big Buildings," delivered at a conference: Learning from the Mall of America: The Design of Consumer Culture, Public Life, and the Metropolis at the End of the Century, held at the University of Minnesota, Minneapolis, November 22, 1997.

9   Gehry joined Victor Gruen after graduation and left only after he felt he could no longer advance within the firm. Alex Wall, unpublished interview with Frank Gehry, May 14, 1998.

10 Nancy Rivera Brooks, "The Mall Face-Lift Craze," *Los Angeles Times*, February 10, 1990, D1; Kenneth J. Garcia, "The Selling of Malls," *Los Angeles Times*, December 27, 1990, J1.

11 See, for example, Theodore Adorno, "Cultural Criticism and Society," *Prisms* (New York: Vintage, 1976).

12 This position is best exemplified by the work of the critic Michael Hays and has been elaborated in the journal he edits, *Assemblage*.

13 See Guy Debord, *Society of the Spectacle*, and Jean Baudrillard, *Simulations* (New York: Semiotext(e), 1983). In spite of their common conclusion that the "real" has now been subsumed by the reproduction, these two theorists differ absolutely in their attitudes towards this transformation. Debord, the modernist, deplores it while Baudrillard revels in what he calls the "hyperreal."

Universal City, California, USA.

Canal City Hakata, Fukuoka, Japan.

Drawings from Jon Jerde's notebooks.

New Port City The unbuilt New Port City project of 1986 is a masterplan for a 400-acre, multiuse urban scheme on a tract of neglected land in Jersey City on the Hudson River, facing Manhattan's Wall Street and the World Trade Center. The 90 million square foot project brings density and variety to an abandoned industrial site.

Page 56: Conceptual site plan.

Left: Watercolor sketch renderings (vignettes) depicting elements of New Port City.

YOU ARE HERE ⇩

In 1986, developer Mel Simon hired the Jerde Partnership to transform the Hudson River pier—400 acres (162 ha.) of crumbling warehouses and freight lines. Simon and co-developer Sam LeFrak had already commissioned a scheme from another firm, one that was conventional: Jerde described it as a "formulaic product with disconnected urban parts." Since the site was connected by tunnel and train to Manhattan, Jerde convinced the developers to define the project not as a suburban development but rather a new district of New York City. He also proposed to demonstrate that by recombining the same catalogue of parts—office buildings, shopping, houses and apartment buildings—they could breathe life into the project. "Rather than a hotel sitting in the middle of an asphalt parking lot, five department stores, and the requisite glass-block office building, all sitting on a straight stretch of road, the parts could be layered to create a pedestrian-related, but automobile-based, community— a neighborhood," Jerde argued. The developers agreed, and within a day a design team had taken over a derelict loading dock on the site and moved in, sealing up the openings with plastic. Fifteen people worked for fifteen days and produced a detailed plan for a 90 million square foot (8.4 million s.m.) development.

The program was dense: harbors, waterfronts, yacht clubs, exhibition and trade marts, low- and high-rise residential, financial and corporate office districts, retail, hotels, nightclub districts, museums and cultural components. Its "vast menu of uses was very compact," describes Jerde. "By using canals, parking as topography, and a shifting uniform grid we created a place of intense variety."

The New Port City plan includes a spiraling water transportation system driven by the rise and fall of the Hudson River tide. Jerde often integrates into projects what he calls "freebies": low-tech, natural phenomena that can be used to produce monumental effects (for example, wind-propelled sailboats, Egyptian sunlight manipulations, gravity railroads, tidal transportation systems). The New Port City plan proposed holding the water in cistern tanks to generate energy in a gravity-run system.

The project's urban core surrounds a marina bifurcated by a canal system that winds in upon itself to culminate at a commercial core. This core is linked to a three-level pier containing a hotel and shops. To preserve the vistas of Manhattan's towers, structures along the waterfront are kept low, rising to taller commercial, mixed-retail and residential zones at the rear.

Below: Sketch of celebratory space designed for the center of New Port City.

"Humankind was disengaged from the whole by the effects of modern design. Cities were ruptured; singular structures unrelated to their context were built, damaging the cohesive and complex urban experience. Now we must be communally pro-survival; only win—win goals allowed." Jon Jerde

Below: Sketch by Jon Jerde
illustrating New Port City's
relationship to Manhattan.

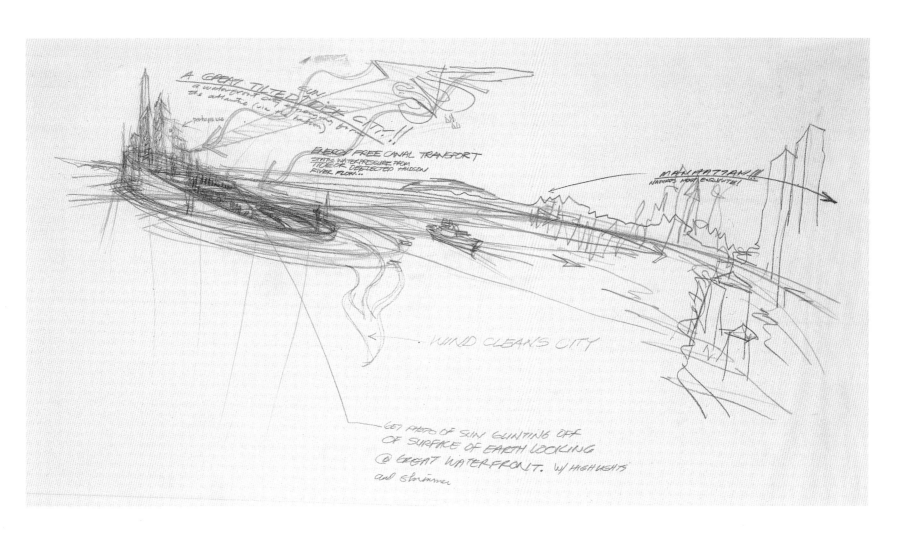

Coupvray

T.G.V.

N 34

YA

F 3

(ZA)

AE

Hu

Tu

COUPVRAY

Support

Employee
Parking

Guest Parking

B

CHESSY

Support

X

ZD

W 2

Guest Parking

Satellite New Town In 1985 the Jerde Partnership designed a scheme for one of the new satellite cities planned around Paris. The diagrammatic solution consisted of a shallow dome rising out of the verdant green plane of the surrounding countryside, with roads and alleys designed in concentric and radiating paths. This shallow, metaphorical earth-dome served as a progenitor to the Universal City Masterplan in Los Angeles.

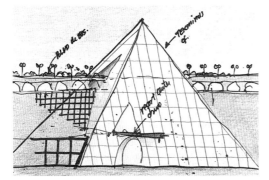

Page 60: Conceptual site plan.

Left: Sketch rendering.

Below: Diagram illustrating the "city roof."

Bottom: Drawings from Jerde's sketchbooks.

YOU
ARE
HERE
⇩

A US-based entertainment company had obtained the rights to develop a 6,000-acre (2,430 ha.) new town. The 1.5 million square foot (139,000 s.m.) project would serve as the home base for visitors to a theme park. The design was to be an European showcase, with culture and amusement zones, entertainment, retail, an international design center, hotels, spas and a conference center. The project had to be sufficiently compelling to interest visitors for about three days.

The Jerde Partnership attempted to create a latter-day utopian suburb by marrying the density and richness of nearby Paris with the pastoral beauty of the countryside. The plan consists of an array of districts, each with a different character, function and theme, subdivided by a network of varied streets, interwoven with landscape.

Although diagrammatic, this new city was designed as a self-contained universe, both in program and metaphor. "It was to be built in one phase rather than to grow organically over time," explains Jerde. "Thus I felt the whole city should have a singular iconic quality. This was to be a city as a metaphor for the Earth." He calls the sloped scheme a "city roof—a living roof of plants and wheat fields, flowers and roads." Conceptually, the project is a "discus that contains memories and fragments of the planet, rainforests, and realms dedicated to a place, culture or time."

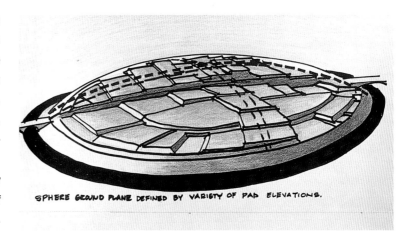

SPHERE GROUND PLANE DEFINED BY VARIETY OF PAD ELEVATIONS.

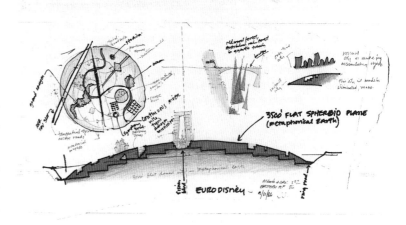

"We are trying to build the metaphor for the Earth." Jon Jerde

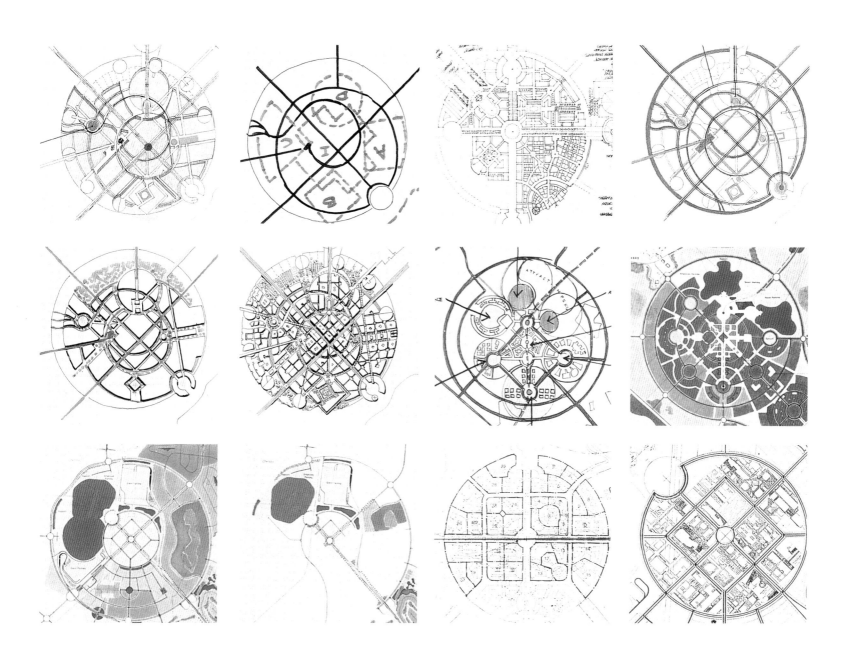

Above: Series of diagrams
illustrating the development
of the masterplan.

Satellite New Town, Near Paris, France

Below: Detailed conceptual
sketch rendering, indicating
division of the site.

Bottom: Section view.

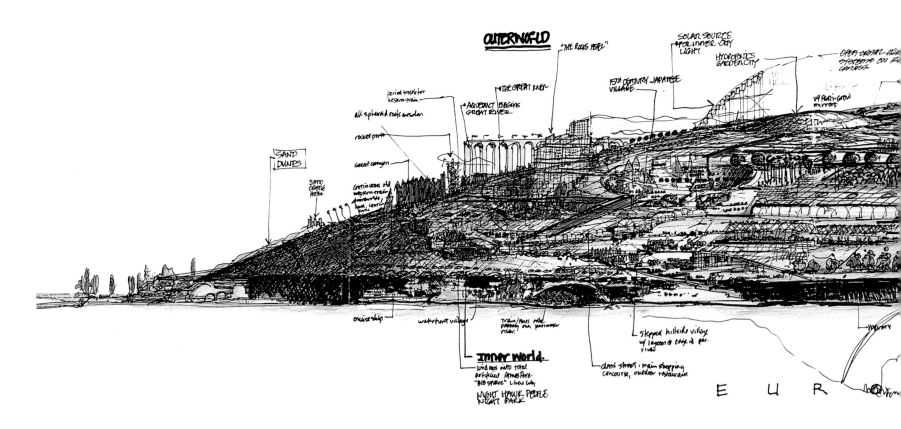

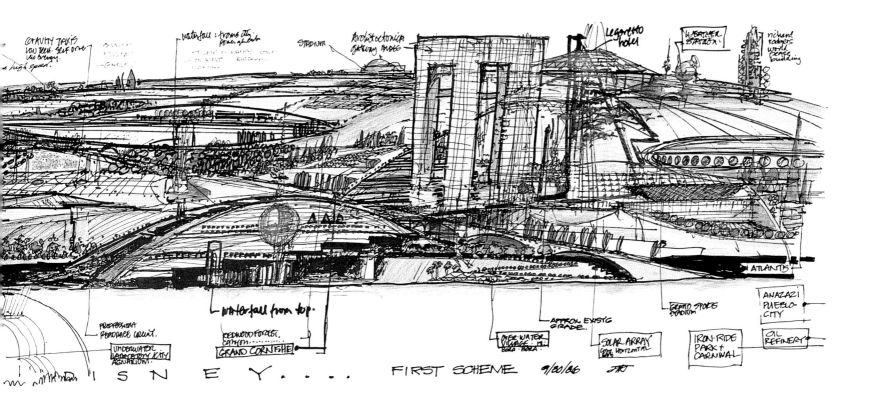

FIRST SCHEME   9/20/86

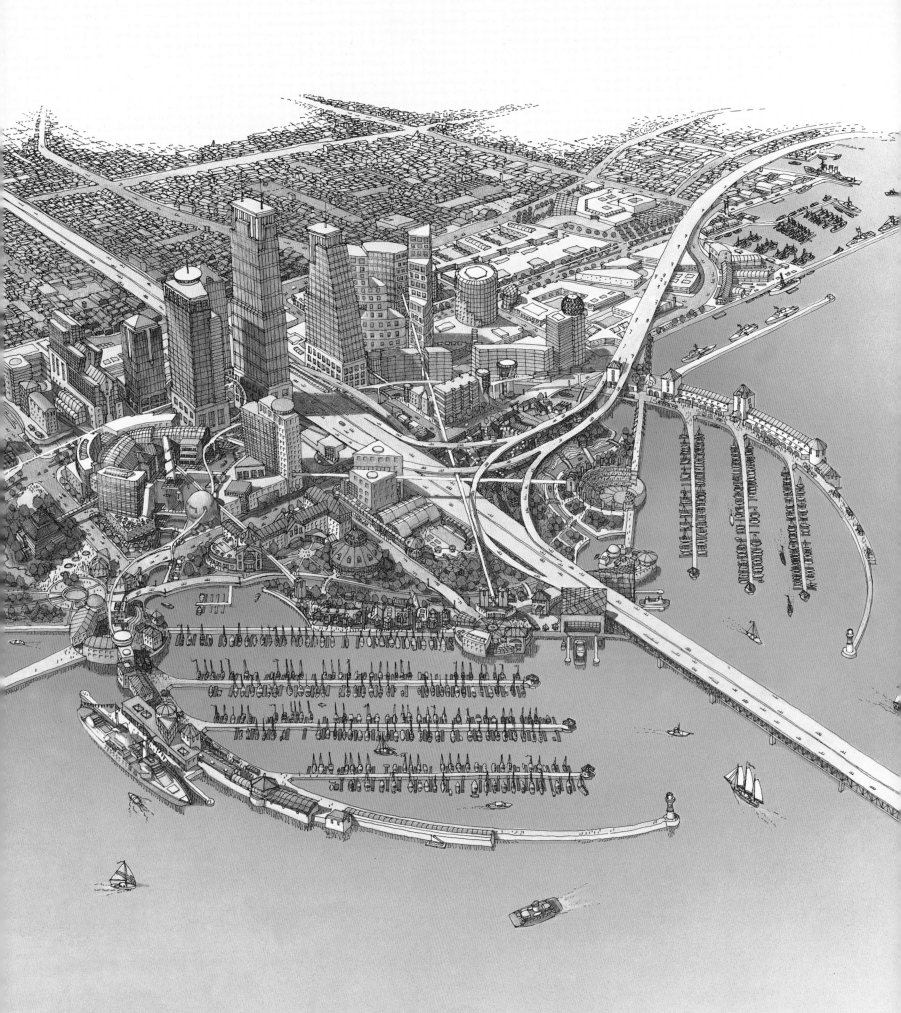

Rinku Masterplan and Town Block III Designed in 1989 for Osaka Bay in Japan, the Rinku Town masterplan is an unbuilt scheme for a new mixed-use, urban district with retail, entertainment and cultural uses. At the core of the district is a mixed-use development called Rinku Town Block III. Occupying 10.7 acres of the total 75-acre plan, this has an eight-story "parkscape," designed to celebrate the union of air, land and water.

YOU
ARE
HERE
⇩

"Our work attempts to find the balance between man touching nature and nature touching man." Jon Jerde

With the opening of the Kansai International Airport on a manmade island in Osaka Bay, the Osaka Prefectural Government was committed to the development of a new "metropolis" on 700 acres (280 ha.) of landfill adjacent to the shore. This new district, Rinku Town, would be connected by motorway, rail and water taxi to the airport and to downtown Osaka. The existing masterplan was a rectangular grid of blocks, typical of global airport cities.

The Jerde Partnership was commissioned to design the mixed-use Rinku Town Block III. However, the firm also reworked the masterplan to incorporate interior canals, bays and tributaries that, according to Jon Jerde, "reflect the water-borne nature of the place."

The eight-story Rinku Town Block III combines commercial and cultural components, such as a museum for Japanese art. Its landscaped surface area, or "outer world," covers its subterranean "inner world" of retail and entertainment. A winding pathway takes the visitor through fantasy worlds, inspired by Leonardo Da Vinci's Codex on water. Different kinds of waterfall (ribbon fall, sheet fall, rope fall, white water chaos) are interspersed along the pathway. The walk descends to the city plane, and ends in a gigantic whirlpool. The walk is mirrored below, allowing for the penetration of natural light to the inner world.

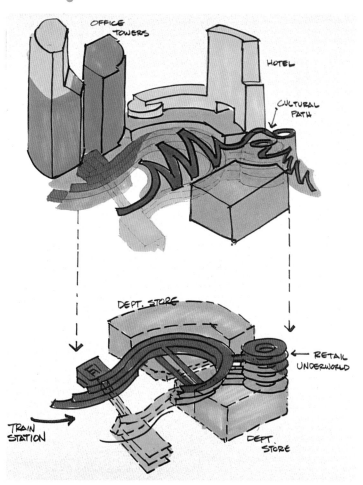

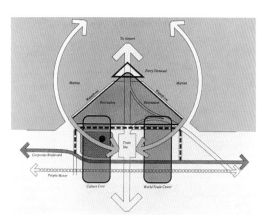

Left: Masterplan diagram.

Above: Block III diagrams showing park plane (top) and retail circulation routes.

Above: Rendered section of Block III.

Rinku Masterplan and Town Block III, Osaka, Japan

Below: Painting of Block III plan
by Jon Jerde.

Opposite: Rendered aerial view
of Block III.

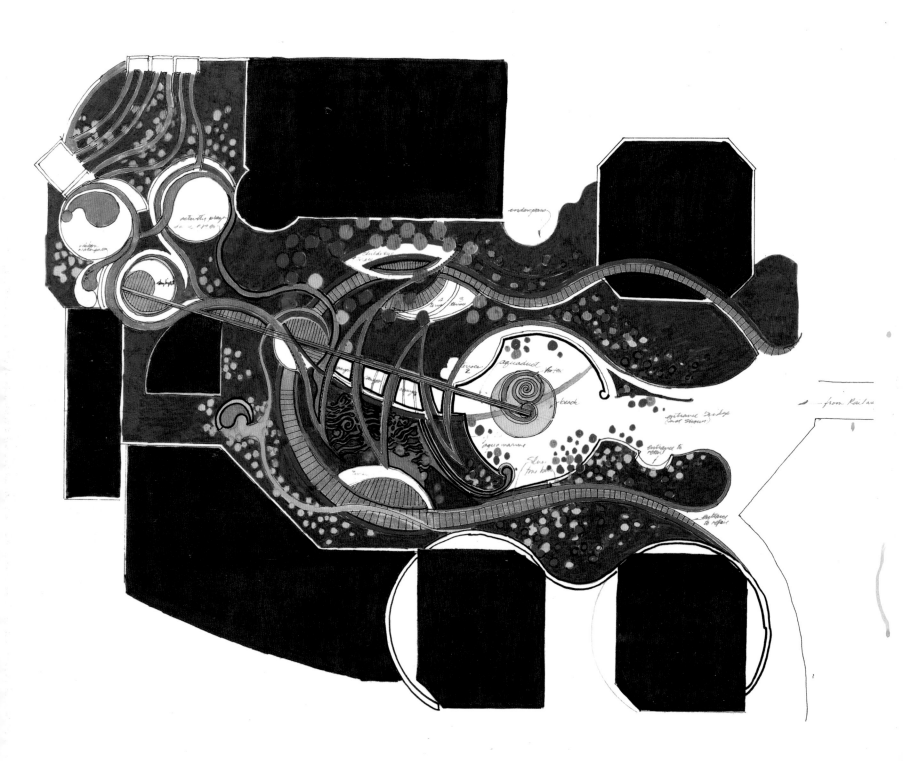

Del Mar Plaza is built into a hillside on a site formerly occupied by a small, obsolete strip shopping center. Overlooking the sea in a seaside town north of San Diego, the 1989 project serves as the center of Del Mar. It has been conceived as a stepping hillside village, inspired by Tuscan hill towns, where both the form and materiality of ageless buildings cause the village to appear to emerge organically on the top of a hill.

YOU
ARE
HERE
⇩

Del Mar Plaza emulates and expands upon European town-planning models. The 75,000 square foot (6,900 s.m.) project is carved into the hillside and is a natural extension of the site and the surrounding village.

Just as traditional circulation patterns in hill towns follow their topography, this project cuts through the incline in a scissorlike path, stopping on each level at open terraces that echo the intimate scale of the seaside town. This path ends at a top-level plaza. Jon Jerde describes the circulation as "a strip shopping center wound up on itself."

The site, which was originally pierced by a commercial highway, contained individual uses serving the community but it had no sense of destination or cohesive qualities. Designed like a European agora, the upper plaza is the heart of the project and has naturally evolved to become Del Mar's main public square.

The architectural language of the place is inspired by Del Mar itself. It is an eclectic mix of eccentric rock work and buildings of a mixed variety of intent; Spanish-roofed Mexican revival houses, wood-and-shingle beach houses, and the ubiquitous Southern California stucco building.

Del Mar Plaza also draws its design idiom from the vernacular Californian Craftsman style. There is a seamless flow between the project's inside and outside, to connect the natural to the manmade. Materials are used in their natural state, including river rock coursed into brick and rough, heavy timbers.

Del Mar is entirely effective as a faux hill town: after wandering through its leafy terraces and paved alleys, the parking garage is found to be concealed in the hill, like the dressing rooms in the back of a theater.

"We deal in the art of the ordinary, we yearn for a marriage between the magic and the banal." Jon Jerde

Above: Aerial view of site.

Below: Rendered watercolor section.

From bottom center, clockwise:
Views to Pacific Ocean from
upper plaza.

Terrace of sun-shaded tables on
upper plaza.

Circulation using local materials
(brick and tile).

Water feature and awning on
upper plaza.

A Craftsman-style awning for
sun protection.

Pages 76–77: View of front
facade from street level.

Luminaire The unbuilt Luminaire project of 1989 was conceived for George Lucas and Skywalker Development as the first of a new generation of entertainment-driven retail projects. Intended to revitalize Houston's core, the project shed the standard department-store anchors in favor of live entertainment venues. Its theme is illumination, deriving form from the play of light.

Left: Rendered view of facade
showing electronically
illuminated skin of Lumisphere.

YOU
ARE
HERE
⇩

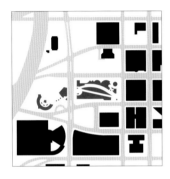

Filmmaker George Lucas, creator of the *Star Wars* trilogy and many other Hollywood blockbusters, was dissatisfied with the presentation of his films. He and his development team intended to create a cinema complex with different-sized auditoriums, with each set up for the perfect optical and aural presentation of a specific film. Lucas also intended to enhance the project with food, attractions and retail.

Located on Houston's historic Buffalo Bayou, a leisure and recreational greenbelt that meanders through the city, Luminaire is designed as a sequence of permanent and temporary environments that uses highly differentiated light as architecture and environmental graphics as landscape. Luminaire would be a "district of light" and metamorphose at dusk into an illuminated cityscape.

The Jerde Partnership created a catalogue of "bolt-on" lighting elements to transform featureless cinema and retail "boxes." The project included electronic reader-boards, giant video panels, and the identifying feature, a sphere made of "pixels" of light, which could be programmed to shimmer, scintillate and undulate. This 100 foot (30 m.) diameter Lumisphere, with an electronically illuminated skin broadcasting information and images, was the precursor to the light tube of the Fremont Street

"Experiential Design: the closest thing to it is movie making, but we don't have any cameras, we don't have any actors, we don't have any scripts, and we don't have any endings." Jon Jerde

Experience in Las Vegas (see p. 136).

Two very different "streets" were layered into the project, both inspired by Lucas' films. One retail-oriented street is high-tech, drawing imagery from space vehicles. The other, for food and attractions, has an industrial atmosphere, drawing from science-fiction and alien worlds. These both terminated in a "night district"—a venue to locate restaurants, bars and clubs opening onto Buffalo Bayou. This night district was a collage of used oil field and oil refinery parts: spheres, tubes, open metal walkways, pipes and valves. Its metal floor would continuously emit a foglike steam, created to allow kinetic penetrations of light, lasers and projections.

Right: Detailed rendered section.

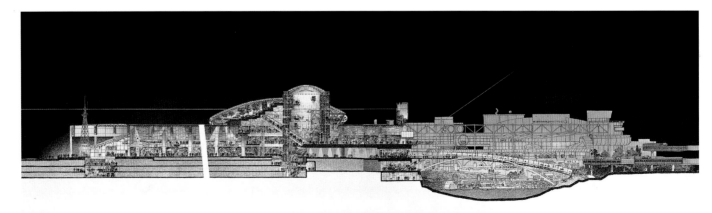

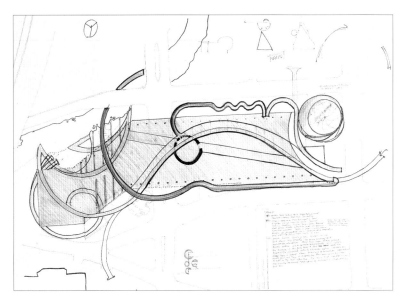
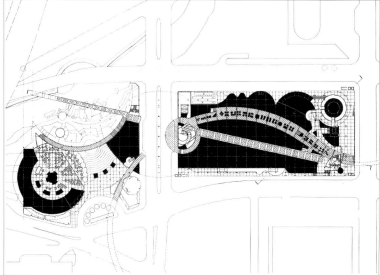
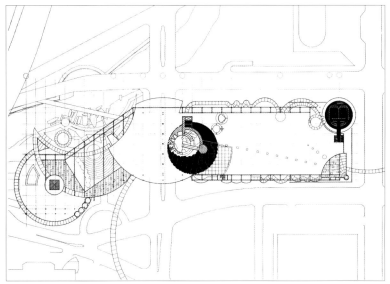
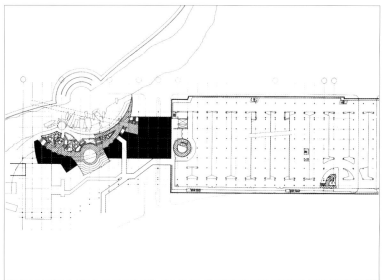
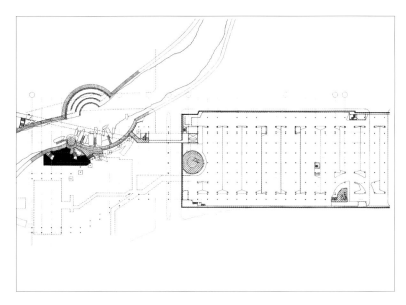
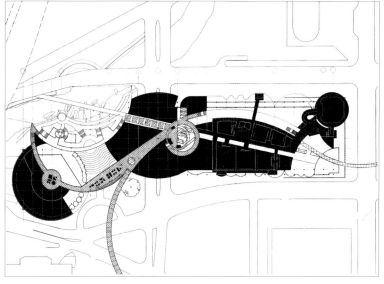

Above left: Drawing from Jon
Jerde's sketchbooks.

Above: Diagrammatic plans of
levels 1–5 of the Luminaire project.

Fashion Island is a renovated regional shopping mall in Newport Beach, California. By introducing urban character to this outmoded 87-acre suburban center in 1989, the Jerde Partnership's strategy rescaled and increased the density of the project by turning wide, axial circulation routes into smaller, winding pedestrian alleys, streets and colonnades. The original shopping complex became a human-scale, landscaped "village," with airy colonnades, sun-dappled paseos, fountains and mosaic paving, which draws its aesthetic references from Spanish Colonial architecture.

Below: Conceptual diagram of masterplan; Fashion Island is Phase One.

Right: Conceptual site plan.

In 1967 Fashion Island was in its prime; center of a state-of-the-art commercial "campus" overlooking Newport Harbor and the Pacific Ocean. Twenty years later, the vast shopping complex, with echoing internal plazas and extra-wide concourses, was upstaged by the new South Coast Plaza, one of the largest assemblages of luxury shops, department stores and cinemas in California. The Irvine Development Company approached the Jerde Partnership to design a $100 million renovation of the 6.3 million square foot (585,000 s.m.) site (the renovation of a JC Penney on the site was not included in the brief).

"The original complex was vastly out of scale, so we created a series of small 'bolt-ons' that, when inserted into the open spaces between buildings, would transform the circulation, creating a 'main street,' side streets and alleys," explains Jerde. This nonorthogonal circulation included porticoed paths linked to small plazas with water features. New sidewalk cafes and colonnades were added, as well as two levels of boutiques, cafes and a cinema complex, and exterior facades provided panoramic ocean views. The renovation is Phase One of the masterplan for Fashion Island. Phase Two "decks over" the vast sea of parking surrounding the center, providing a development podium for multiuse components.

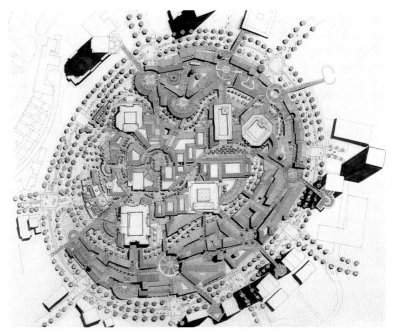

"The shopping center could again be an urban experience, a communal setting that renewed a public life of richness and complexity." Jon Jerde

Right: Sketch study of internal facade.

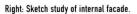

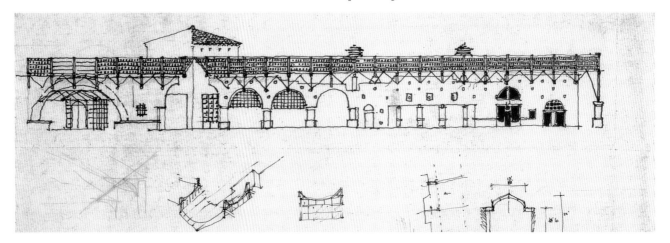

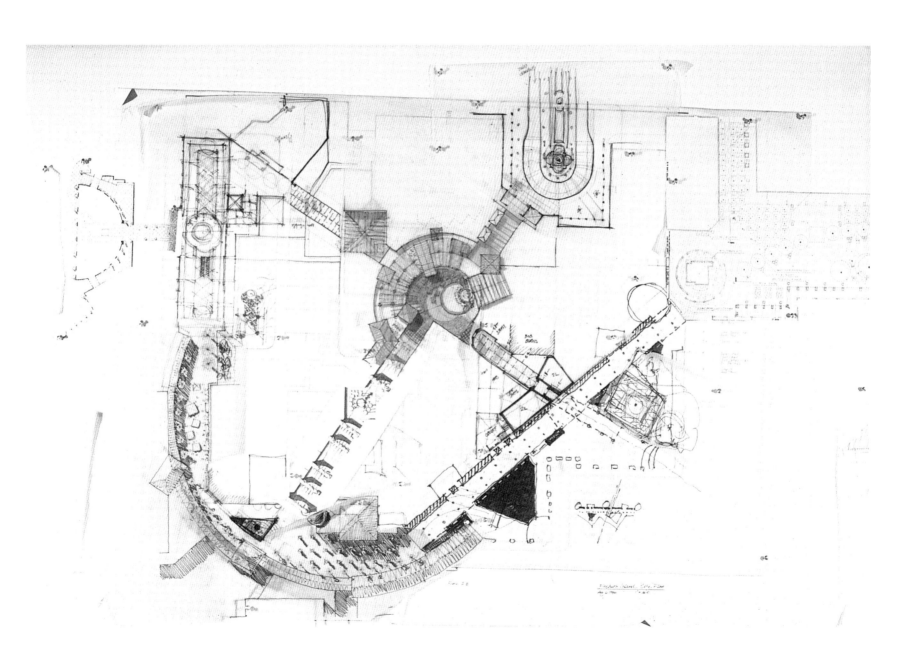

Opposite: Fountain in internal corridor.

This page, below left, bottom left and center: Views of the central fountain court.

Right and below right: Arches and trellised pathways define the internal spaces.

flying machine

monorail

auto bridges

BIKE CABS

Urbanopolis was commissioned by the Wrather Corporation and the Disney Development Company for Anaheim, California in 1990. It was envisioned as a microcosmic city of hotels, restaurants, shopping and entertainment venues. Sited just south of Disneyland, the project was designed primarily to accommodate visitors to the theme park. Urbanopolis was to incorporate a set of amenities to complement Disney's themed environments.

YOU
ARE
HERE
⇩

Opposite: Watercolor sketches of
the cultural fragments that make
up the project.

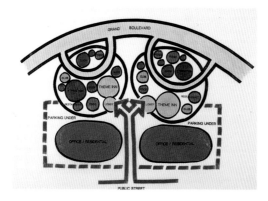

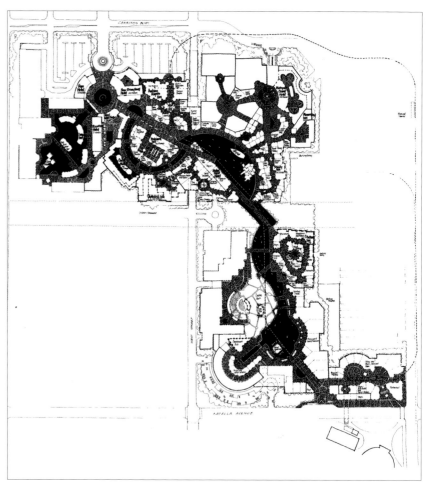

Jerde's clients knew that the hotels, motels and restaurants that surround Disneyland were successful as a result of the millions of visitors generated by the park. The derelict land surrounding Disneyland would be better utilized, in Jerde's words, "if a project was conceived to allow Disney to benefit from all of the visitors that otherwise use the surrounding facilities owned by others."

Noting that Disneyland is a series of "lands" (Fantasyland, Tomorrowland, Adventureland and Frontierland), Jerde proposed a monumental gateway to Urbanopolis called Realityland. Urbanopolis is a collection of cultural fragments—Italian hill town, Chinatown, Arabian Nights, Japanese village—with an uptown and a downtown. Each zone would have a hotel, shops, restaurants and clubs.

"When I look for urban archetypes they are not things, they are sequences." Jon Jerde

Above left: Diagram showing elements of plan and the relationships with existing infrastructure.

Above: Conceptual plan of Urbanopolis.

Makuhari Town Center is an unbuilt leisure center for a new town outside Tokyo in which the Jerde Partnership creates a self-contained universe in an experimental platonic form: a sphere inside a cube. The 1993 project consists of leisure-related retail shops, community rooms, health facilities, restaurants and a television studio.

**YOU
ARE
HERE**
⇩

"When opposites are joined, a continuum is defined. The creation of a continuum is important because it initiates complexity and provides a vessel inside which anything can happen." Jon Jerde

The Jerde Partnership was hired by Mitsubishi Real Estate to create an entertainment hub for the residents of Makuhari that would operate as the town's center, comprising retail, health facilities, restaurants—with the unusual addition of television studios.

The concept for Makuhari Town Center is that of a journey that can be divided vertically with its source at the base, a resting zone in the middle, and the destination at the top. The source, an antichamber where visitors gather to begin this journey, is the heart and meeting place of the town center. The middle zone is a resting place for contemplation of the world above and below. Above is a futuristic entertainment district. As Jerde describes it, "the bottom half reflects the terrestrial world of earth, land-scape and water, and the top half is a representation of the celestial world of clouds, stars and sky."

Four exterior towers also reflect the terrestrial/ celestial metaphor. They undergo a transition from the solid earth—the bases are stone—to a light, plant-filled membrane above.

While the interior is a self-contained universe, externally the project refers to its surroundings, with each of the facades tailored to its adjacent context. The north and east facades are local in scale, with a pedestrian street, while on the south facade a grand entry and forecourt express the building's regional role. Set back from the street, the west facade is a super-scale composition responding to an adjacent open plaza.

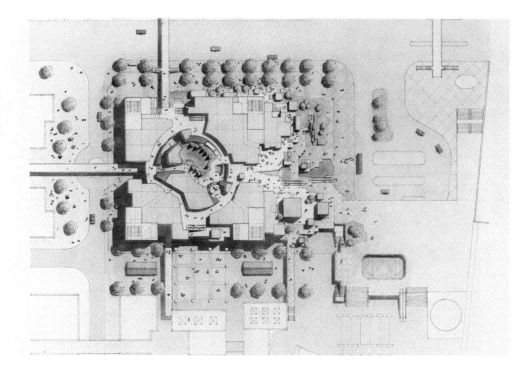

Left: Rendered site plan showing connections to the existing urban fabric.

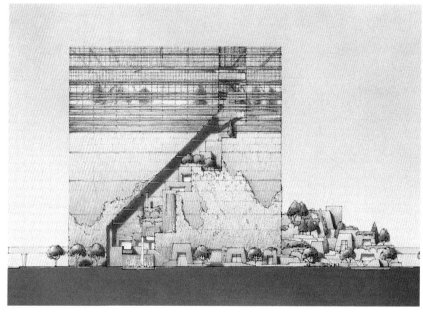

This page: Rendered elevations of Makuhari, exploring the different qualities of the adjacent city fabric.

Left: Rendered perspective
section of the interior world,
external shell and surrounding
context.

Mall of America is the Goliath of shopping malls. An average of 40 million people visit this self-contained shopping and entertainment center each year, the largest in America. At 4.2 million square feet, Mall of America is the size of seven Yankee Stadiums. More than 400 stores, 71 restaurants, a 14-screen movie complex, and an aquarium surround the largest indoor theme park in the nation, Knott's Berry Farm's Camp Snoopy. Built in Bloomington, Minneapolis, in 1992, and designed to simulate a city, Mall of America is the first, and arguably still the clearest, hybrid of retail and entertainment in America.

YOU
ARE
HERE
⇩

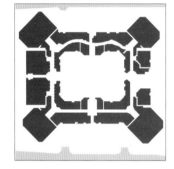

Mall of America is on a vast suburban site formerly occupied by Minneapolis' Met Stadium. Designed by the Jerde Partnership as a world-within-a-world, its weather-controlled environment offers a retreat from the freezing Minneapolis climes and a convenient three-hour layover for travelers passing through the nearby Minneapolis/St. Paul airport.

Mall of America replicates the urban and the natural in an enclosed universe. Here one can finish high school (176 students were enrolled in Mall of America High School in 1997), go to college and, in the Chapel of Love, tie the knot (1,000 weddings were performed at the Chapel of Love in its first five years). The natural is replicated, also, with "rocks" cast from cliffs along the St. Croix River, and more than four hundred trees growing under 1.2 miles of skylights. Visitors can also play a round of golf on a two-level, miniature-golf mountain.

Mall of America is anchored by four large department stores connecting "streets" that are divided into four distinctive shopping districts, each of which is punctuated by an activity area at the center that opens into the 7-acre (2.8 ha.) Knott's Berry Farm's Camp Snoopy theme park. The character of each street varies from the landscaped North Garden to West Market, an "international marketplace." South Avenue offers upscale retail while East Broadway is a contemporary, "high-energy" venue. An entertainment district on Level Four, East Broadway, is a collage of cafes and restaurants, each a mini-theme park unto itself.

Spatial complexity is created vertically in each of the districts by the layering of a circular plan at the third and fourth levels over a square plan at the first and second levels. "These kinds of experiential complexities were necessary," explains Jon Jerde, "to bring some sense of a memorable geography: a walk through the project is four and a half miles long."

"In America the last vestiges of community are a parade, a football game and a shopping center."

Jon Jerde

Left: Sketches illustrating "memorable geography."

Opposite: Sketches showing the interior as an enclosed "village" (above) and under glass canopy (below).

Mall of America, Bloomington, Minnesota, USA

This page: Plans of four different
retail levels showing retail
anchors.

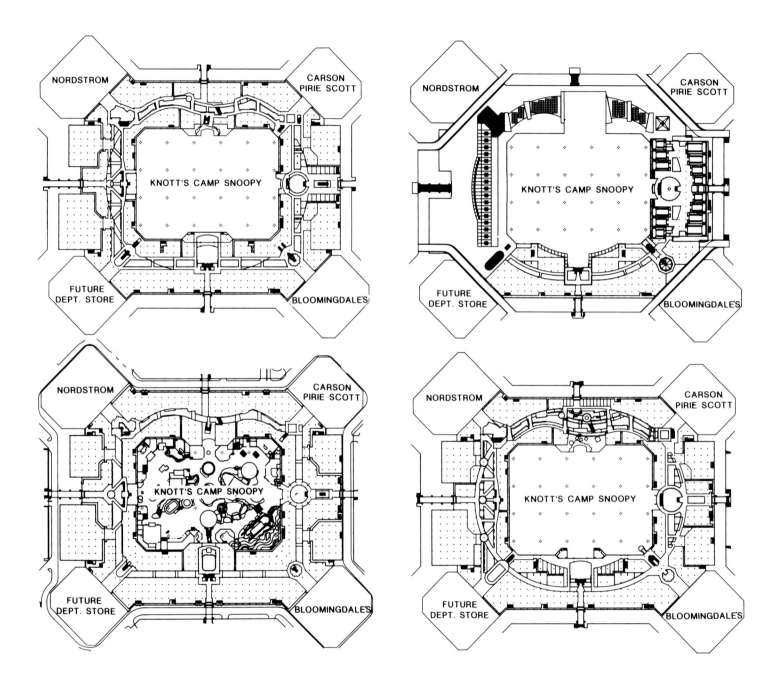

This page: Early rendered sections
showing activity and landscaping.

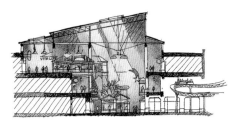

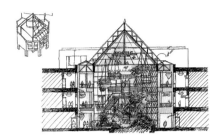

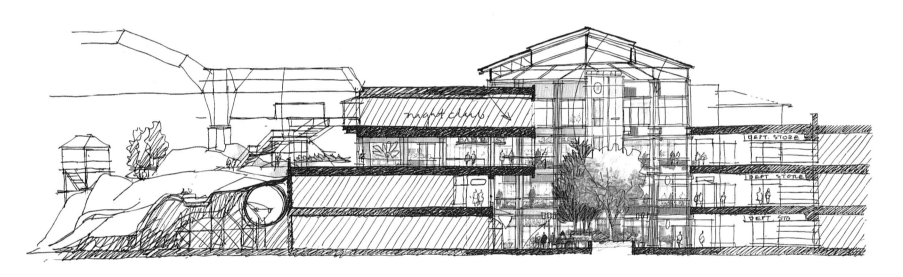

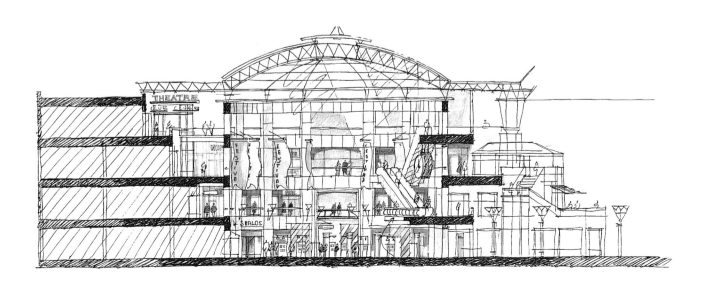

This page and opposite: Views of the interior of the mall, including the enclosed theme park.

Pages 106–7: Knott's Berry Farm's Camp Snoopy is enclosed by four levels of retail units.

Rokko Island is a manmade island in Kobe's harbor that blends urban and natural environments to create a multifunctioning marine city. Reached by a causeway connected to the mainland, the 1992 project is intended to function as a new district of the city with retail, entertainment, office, housing and convention hotel uses. It is also a "techno-village," or vehicle for demonstrating a range of technological endeavors. Jerde's concept of "veneer ecology" produced five blocks of development with high-density towers and detached dwellings, all contained within a vast tilted plane facing the sea.

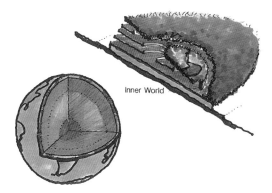

Inner World

Left: Sketch diagrams explaining "veneer ecology."

Opposite: Rendered view of central plaza.

YOU
ARE
HERE
⇩

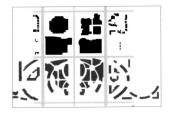

"The challenge is to trigger — to inspire — unity. . . ." Jon Jerde

The Jerde Partnership injected complexity into the Rokko masterplan that, in Jerde's view, is essential to the successful creation of place. This complexity "derives from the interconnection and overlap of many different circulation patterns into an 'urban tapestry.'" Each circulation pattern is choreographed in a different way to provide multiple experiences. The Rokko Island geometry combines an ellipse with a circle and a square, all grouped about a spine, or armature. A four-level pedestrian shopping and dining arcade is a figure-eight in plan, reinforcing the north–south axis of the site. It intertwines with the existing linear pedestrian mall, culminating at a large plaza, which is surrounded by an office building and a convention hotel. On the level above is the Mart Arc, the secondary organizer that unites the various districts of the project. The square Sky Block is a third-level city block that contains mostly evening attractions—cinemas, nightclubs, electric street and museum.

To unify this complex project, the firm proposes an ecological concept—veneer ecology—in which the site has a thin veneer of gardens and parkscape. This park, Rokko Terrace, is designed as a green, living landscaped layer— a metaphorical microcosm of the earth's greater surface—oriented to the south and toward the sea. The sea enters the project on its central axis, symbolically imparting life to the island.

At the core of the Rokko Island masterplan is the "urban resort center," designed to overlap diverse leisure uses connected by bridges and pathways.

Right: Diagrammatic site plan showing intersecting circulation patterns.

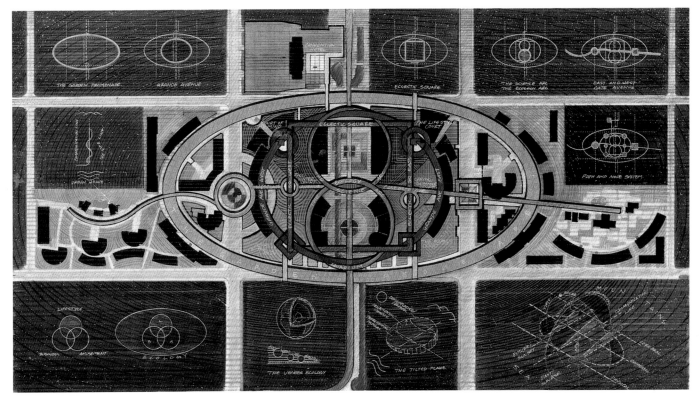

The Electronic Baroque: Jerde Cities Norman M. Klein

The twentieth century ended in 1989, once the Wall came down. Afterward, from one continent to another, a strange blend of grotesquely primitive formations emerged, from Bosnian nightmares to warlord capitalism. At the same time, a genteel extreme emerged as well: the largest McDonald's in the world was built in Moscow; suites for Korean high-rollers appeared in Las Vegas. The contrasts are staggering, and yet somehow ergonomic, for a world dominated increasingly by a new kind of corporate monopoly. Huge, newly enlarged (or even engorged) corporations are held together essentially by advertising campaigns and digital media—very much by an "easy-listening" model of power.

For cities caught inside these emerging contrasts, the Jerde Partnership has taken a unique role, as the builder of new paradigms "on every continent except Antarctica." As Jerde said, the city is condensed into "toy towns" with "casbahs." The patina of old city markets is accelerated into a single building cycle. Indeed, the shopping center of the early Cold War has matured into a full blown city of sorts. But what kind is that? Like late medieval cities, it has expanded beyond its walls and entered city streets themselves. The outdoor shopping near the old mall in Burbank, California, has sprawled, as has Jerde's Horton Plaza into the turn-of-the-century Gaslamp District across the street.

This process can be compared to Baroque cities of the seventeenth and eighteenth centuries—after the old medieval walls were removed. In spaces beyond the walls or the palace grounds, sculptural fantasies were added. In the electronic Baroque today, global franchise capitalism blends with movie fantasies and suburbanism blends with nostalgia for an industrial city that has disappeared. As the mall has evolved into urban planning, we inhabit a world where entertainment and the world economy merge.

At the center of the electronic Baroque is illusion as a "scripted space," where the walk is designed carefully, not unlike the levels on a computer game. Bernini helps us understand the purpose of these phantasmagoria. "To make of Time a thing stupendous," he wrote.[1] This could be understood not only as frozen allegory, a movement implied in an animated gesture, but also the pedestrian's time: a walk past the fountain, the altar, under the dome, into the piazza. During this passage, a story unfolds, based on forced perspective, trompe l'œil, what scholars call points of projection. In some cases, like the interiors designed by **Andrea Pozzo**[2] in the early eighteenth century, marble disks were assigned, as vantage points, where the images would wane, reconnect, become more robust.[3] Clearly, this is a kind of walk-through narrative. The paths are theatricalized to encourage "story," but also to glorify the client—the Counter-Reformation or the monarch. The route seems less restricted, but still reminds pedestrians who is in charge, that the duke sanctioned all these choices. It was liberated late feudalism. It met a growing pressure in the seventeenth century, "the peasant population's invasion of the city,"[4] in our terms, a rudimentary mode of consumer culture. Rituals originally for the knightly class were released to the "public."[5]

In a similar spirit, the Jerde spaces are Baroque illusion that privileges the visitor's walk, but also provides well for the corporate client.[6] Instead of seventeenth-century mercantilism, we have franchise mercantilism, dominated by shopping mall developers who are increasingly allowed to plan sections of cities. Of course, how far shall we take this metaphor? The parallels are instructive more than absolute. What if we considered Jerde's work on Bellagio as "absolutist,"[7] where the Las Vegas developer Steve Wynn builds his own Versailles as a tourist hotel?

During Baroque eras, the walls and ceilings became a narrative text expanded from Renaissance devices, like trompe l'œil or anamorphosis. These were conceived very much as a narratized walk through (as in the example from Pozzo). The tradition began in the fifteenth century, essentially with Brunelleschi's architecture and **Mantegna's paintings:** neo-platonic fantasy in churches, palaces, theaters, then extending into piazzas and roads. The narratives relied on englobed, immersive spaces that filtered dynamically from the ceiling. Sculpture alluded often to theater (stage plays).[8] Tableaux vivants allowed visitors to enter narrative almost in the sense of a masque. By the eighteenth century, this gaudy but elegant code had evolved into a design industry. Traveling painters called quadraturista specialized in fantasy illusionism. Handbooks were available on trompe l'œil and anamorphosis,[9] broad surveys on how to paint a scripted space. It had matured into an elaborate grammar—oddly parallel both to film grammar and to the Jerde mall.

However, similar handbooks on the electronic variation of the Baroque are not quite ready yet. Studies on postmodern illusionism abound; they are a subindustry, of course, but are not meant as point-by-point grammars. "**The Disneyland effect**" has entered our language, to remind us that hypertrophied mall "cities" have become essential to globalized tourism. The overlapping tropes from many media at once inspire a tourist sensation without the jet lag. For a few hours, you visit a

Andrea Pozzo, *Allegory of the Missionary Work of the Jesuits*, 1691–94, ceiling of the nave of S. Ignacio, Rome, Italy.

Andrea Mantegna, ceiling of the Camera degli Sposi, Palazzo Ducale, Mantua, Italy.

Andrea Mantegna, detail of *The Agony in the Garden*.

Disneyland, Anaheim, California, USA.

"global" resort for shopping, then drive home. As a corollary, much has been written about the collapse of public space, at least "public" as it was understood in the industrial city of 1920. In other words, our culture is abandoning the rights to assembly on dense streets. The "bughouse squares" where orators used to rally on soapboxes inside parks are gone. Street vending has become a public nuisance in the new suburban city. Indeed, narrative architecture "speaks" on behalf of a different model for public interaction—franchise outlets for imperial businesses from around the world; and local copies of these franchises. We accept that fact, but how should we proceed from there, in mapping out the future of political assembly, shopping between the classes? Malls may not evolve into bughouse squares or into sites for labor rallies.

Jon Jerde asks what public spaces—the plazas, parks, public squares and meeting places—have been built in major cities over the past fifty years? What experience today can compare to the dense street life many of us imagine for Manhattan or Paris, or see in the opening credits to every Sherlock Holmes movie? Indeed, our culture is developing a substitute, what Jerde calls "a community of consumers." This is more stable than philosopher Jean Baudrillard's notion of a precession of dissolving simulacra. Baudrillard describes a disoriented code, copies without originals. What we find instead is something much more stable. Disorienting copies become plot points along the way.

The Jerde city is more like the **story boards** for a movie. Inside this diachronic path, illusions (or simulacra) do not dissolve the story; they serve as plot points in the movie script.

What is the role of the viewer in this sculpted movie? For example, forty years ago, movie glamour implied a visit to a premiere, to be among the cognoscenti who first saw the finished product. Now, increasingly, the movie set itself has replaced the premiere. One is encouraged to shop inside a movie set. The consumer journey literally resembles a film shoot.

More specifically, it resembles a special-effects movie: scripted spaces with illusionistic effects in which the audience is a central character. For example, the Moorish touches at the front of Horton Plaza or **the nineteenth-century arcade** at the spine of the Westside Pavilion are movie sets for a story one walks through, where the shops comment on the scale or the colors or the signifier. This is not a new strategy at all, more like the recovery of older scripted spaces. The consumer, like the Baroque parishioner three hundred years ago, is the central character in a miniaturized epic of sorts; but in personal terms, the story is Weberian. Max Weber wrote about the Protestant ethic merging with the work ethic in Europe.[10] Here we see the tourist culture merging with a consumer-driven personalized daydream. The scripted space is a form of predestination, where the consumer "acts out" the illusion of free will.

Jerde himself uses the term "story" very often, much as Disney did. The story must be different for each visitor. Even though the path is pre-scripted, the journey should seem random. The facades should look slightly haphazard; the scale should be ascending, welcoming. Jerde takes the myth of dense democratic ways very seriously. Even though the lessees, owners and the merchandisers may control the script more than the audience, the myth must be sustained somehow. For example, an immersive, but open-air dome at the center of

CityWalk serves as a piazza for a consumerist republic, as if the Jerde city were a town meeting.

CityWalk embodies this paradox very clearly. It was the first leg of a larger masterplan to integrate hundreds of thousands, even millions of square feet, from the Universal Outdoor Recreation Tours to the MCA office buildings—but first "to link the parking garage and the Tour gate." The theme essentially was to encapsulate Los Angeles, what Jerde calls "the transactual city," LA as a "deal-business" diagram. Urban planning in LA is indeed often a product of Faustian deals concocted over a long lunch, and by unlikely partners. Subway stations appear without subway lines. Infrastructure is auctioned off like overstock at a clothing store. Someone is allowed to stucco over blocks at a time. Someone else chops down century-old maguey and oak, or falls in love with Italianate porticoes or a touch of the Italian Alps. LA reveals the constant war between lush greenery and asphalt. Lately, greenery—or at least landscaping—has done somewhat better. But the remains of fast deals litter the city: streets carved, weirdly, out of old citrus groves; aerospace acreage being retooled, just as weirdly, into sound stages. Here indeed is the world spirit that Jerde condensed into CityWalk. And in that sense, the community of consumers is an invention to suit shopping and real-estate interests. At the same time, his spaces have very broad appeal; eight million visitors to CityWalk in the first year alone, tens of millions now to Horton Plaza. It is easier to imagine what he does as a kind of mercantilism—franchise capitalism as an urban motif, the Baroque glorification of trade. This mercantile fantasy bridges two extremes, from the upscale lemonade stand to a *Blade Runner* ride.

Rocco, Curri, Boubée, Di Mauro, Galleria Umberto I, Napoli, Italy.

Urbanopolis, Anaheim, California, USA.

Universal CityWalk, Universal City, California, USA.

The Script of Citywalk

Jerde claims that **Blade Runner** was part of the inspiration for CityWalk, for example, the cyber-noir use of signage, the sense of overheads into dense crowds. Certainly, the space is laid out like a movie set, in a half circle that is interspersed (according to developer Jim Nelson) by "hot spots," a bench or plants where the circle gets too obvious. Jerde would have a more elegant curve to describe the "between"; that is, the necklace that holds the stores. He is constantly doodling shapes that could be "in between."

Indeed, Jerde has an almost metaphysical fascination with how the zeitgeist of the story is found, as if he were taking a divining rod to find an underground stream. He calls this stream an "armature," shaped like a line that, while artificial, is irrepressibly "natural." We walk through the original CityWalk of 1994, before it was expanded toward a more clearly teenage market (a Hard Rock Café, etc). We start from the parking structure, immediately see the movie complex (the principal moneymaker for Universal, even more than the leases around it). Then we head along the half circle toward the highest point, near the see-through dome, in view of **King Kong** marking the half-way mark. Each miniaturized slice of Los Angeles is punctuated by neon signs salvaged from bulldozed shops and supermarkets around the city, to reinforce the sense of substitution, that this set can absorb the real and the false into a new synthesis. A single facade for UCLA, a pinch of beach for Venice, an ocean machine that sounds real enough up close, a pinch of Melrose; and each out of scale, or in a different material to the original. It is **trompe l'œil** as Baroque interior, as theater "in between" more than architectural facades. Jerde has relo-cated a Baroque to an Art Nouveau tradition that Modernism had rejected, then updated it.

In Jerde's words, he makes "the real look artificial." I am reminded of what Roland Barthes meant by the term mythologies, how the artificial becomes so natural that it cannot be questioned.[11] Of course, Barthes was thinking of corporate ideology. Jerde is operating at the intersection of many ideologies at once: shopping, tourism, real estate, global entertainment—and finally, local myths about the neighborhood (the colonial Mexican San Diego, the rooflines of northern Japan).

Jerde insists that armatures are also a strand of local collective memory. He is almost animistic in his sense that the armature is a collective memory, the flow of "Gaia," the monads of global consciousness; monad here as the global whole shrunk down to a small unit, like the enclosing walls embracing the water in **Canal City Hakata**. He compares the armature to rivers leaving strata on rocks, as if the path of the community of consumers were responding as well to a nativist, genetic code.

The armature is literally curved as if etched by weather. He is convinced today that the unconscious inspiration for Canal City was **Canyon de Chelly**, in Arizona, a canyon running flush with the desert into a "verdant valley" by a river. The rocky face of the canyon has been inscribed by winds for millennia by "spherical wind cusps." And inside the canyon wall, Anasazi Indians had cut a city. Similarly, the two faces of Canal City enclose the canal itself and seem honeycombed, as if shops were cut into stone.

But beyond "making the real look artificial," or as a co-creative impulse from the Partnership to the developer to the community, Jerde also imagines that the armature is a catalyst. It grows beyond its limits "organically." What is more, this growth should be accelerated, to speed a century of urbanization into perhaps ten years, a kind of fast-drying patina. The older shopping centers (1950–80) were not organic, certainly not in touch with the streets around them: "boxes without windows," he calls them. They repeated a masterplan based on industrial efficiency or one-stop shopping, like defense plants or stockyards or supermarkets. In contrast, the Jerde city tries to heroize trophy imagery from the local culture, exaggerate, even parody it. The line of buildings for lease along the armature should encourage local businesses, not simply global franchise, though frankly, wouldn't any local businesses in such a site have to resemble the global anyway, the globalized localism of the electronic Baroque?

But more evident is the look of the space from outside. It opens like a pocket. Jerde shrugs off, good-naturedly, the idea of a slice of melon. He agrees, however, that the bricolage impact of the facade, beginning with his mixing of elements at Horton Plaza, should not appear sealed off. I am reminded of envelopes stuffed into a basket, as forced perspective, games of scale. He often describes the assortment as "kits of parts," and refers to the drawings of "ghostly shapes" by architect Aldo Rossi (again for Horton Plaza in particular). The kit, taken from tourist versions of local imaginaries, assembles shapes that leave the armature (a term he first used when rushing for deadline on Horton Plaza). Horton was a re-assemblage, the building blocks of the linear shopping mall juggled: two towers for department stores, a thread snarled for shops, and then a "rich man's house," with fancy tile work, to interrupt the space further. This Jerde calls "Abbott and Costello

Blade Runner (dir. Ridley Scott, 1982), with Harrison Ford.

CityWalk, Universal City, California, USA.

Francesco Borromini, cupola of S. Ivo alla Sapienza, Rome, Italy.

Canal City Hakata, Fukuoka, Japan.

White House Indian ruins, Canyon de Chelly, Arizona, USA.

at the Casbah."[12] The Jerde Partnership was allowed finally to "pull the top" (no roof), but this was seen as money-saving as well as responding to the gentle climate. Materials had to be inexpensive, "cheap stucco, asphalt and paint" (the entire project came in at only $140 million). The colors resemble the palette by designers Sussman/Prezja that Jerde applied to the LA Olympics. But most of all, the area was presumably too cheap for upscale investment, the side of Broadway no one wanted to visit or lease, "a burnt-out town." The builder Ernest Hahn would explain that only 5000 inhabitants lived there, "half of them addicts, half of them fish."

Thus Jerde was asked to consider Horton Plaza as a redevelopment project. He decided to make it a "condensed San Diego" with room to grow into the Gaslamp Quarter nearby. The space had to allow "the jewelry of the street to keep changing."

The result has a picturesque density, modeled partly as well on **Italian hill towns** (Monte Fiasconi, Jerde explains). I am always reminded of a colorful ant farm, layer by layer, striated in yet another way. Of course, Horton Plaza became an immense success, attracting 25 million visitors in the first year.

Within a decade of its appearance, by the mid-1990s, the Gaslamp Quarter nearby had expanded, and in fact, began to copy the technicolors of Horton Plaza. In effect, as in cinematic special effect, the real was made artificial. To complete this paradox, the density and bricolage of a city street made safe for consumers as a toy town—a playful town, with inside jokes for the locals, games with scale for the outsider.

Condensed City

The "condensed city" is a term that Jerde uses, but applies fundamentally to the movie set, to the way a New York street on the Paramount lot can combine three parts of Manhattan and a part of Brooklyn within a few hundred meters. But let us for a moment understand condensed as what is left out as well. It can be compared to Freud's notion of condensation, the instantaneous layering of many memories at once, in order to allow the desire to cathect painlessly, to keep the dreamer from awaking. It is urban *chiaroscuro*, for the community of consumers: a condensed, narratized substitution for what must be left out. It is designed experience for a world where audiences prefer to eat inside the movie, rather than simply go to the premiere.

In that sense, condensed also reminds me of the movie miniature, of stop-motion animation, of gentle matte paintings of the end of the world, of *trompe l'œil* murals. The scale must appear condensed, the perspective forced, to allow us to sense what is missing, be charmed by what Jerde calls "the space without space … globality merging into a singular place … the globe simultaneously and instantaneously." The mergers between entertainment and investment are condensed, as is the mutation of suburbs into city streets. Indeed, any street in the Gaslamp Quarter (circa 1900) can become an annex of Horton Plaza, because the walls have disappeared to some degree.

Metropolitan Suburb

The Jerde city is a condensed version of what I call a metropolitan suburb; that is, a Baroque city honoring the new form of mercantilism, the new salvation for ailing cities: franchise tourism with a touch of the local. Indeed, we are now suburban-izing our downtowns, but a highly advanced suburbia. Consumer-driven malls have replaced the 1950s model for shopping centers linked to industrial planning for freeways, for example. New freeways do not direct the suburban sprawl all that much any more, they are not simply bedroom communities twenty minutes from the real jobs. Many postwar suburbs in Southern California, in particular, have evolved into complex cities, with their own financial base, their own slums, their own pedestrian centers. But the roots are still as suburban; very little de-industrialization, very tiny downtowns, if any at all. They are franchise centers with their own gravity. The **Los Angeles** residential suburb of Burbank, California, for example, now controls almost $3 billion a year in media business alone, and is headquarters for the two largest communications giants in the United States. Burbank has indeed spilled its banks as a bedroom community.

CityWalk announced the coming of age of Universal City as a metropolitan suburb. It stands at the center of a series of suburbs that are now themselves media capitals. How appropriate in the era of the electronic Baroque to have the themed space convert into epic cityscape. The movie set as a city has become the new paradigm for urban planning throughout the world. Other townships try to "thematize" their suburban boulevards, to design communities for consumers, and keep that tax base close to home.

Often Jerde is given commissions to redesign in a metro-suburban way the shells of downtowns that have faded into near oblivion (Kansas City, Rotterdam, **Las Vegas**, Phoenix, San Diego). In the USA certainly, these are imagined as cities of the 1920s. The *moderne* architecture of the 1920s

Suburbs, Los Angeles, California, USA.

Universal CityWalk, Universal City, California, USA.

"Before" the Fremont Street Experience, Las Vegas, Nevada, USA.

Urbino, Italy.

cityscape reminds the metro-suburbanite of streets that the middle class has abandoned and now exoticizes. To the powers that be, even to the middle class, the 1920s downtown has begun to resemble Roman ruins, something to rehab until it is slightly upside down. As an electronic Baroque architect, Jerde remakes them as "folly," a quirky pastiche, the spider silk of the pre-World War II streets as an armature, as a condensed movie set for a community of consumers. In the future, any seventeenth- or eighteenth-century city (Prague or Old Stockholm) may be converted into electronic tourist communities as well, simply by readjusting **"the jewelry of the street."** In a few more decades, we will find relatively little of the older industrial city left, except as zones of neglect. If a street has not been rescripted as a community for consumers, it may not be able to support itself, and will drift away or be ignored.

Indeed, the condensed city also represents a culture of distraction—more about what is left out—as the widening class structure finds its institutional forms, like the Jerde city. Of course, Jerde is not the developer or the sociologist. Instead, almost as a formalism, Jerde offers us the grammar. It is for us to locate complexity within that grammar. The scripted space resembles movie sets, applies **Baroque traditions**, mimics urban politics, and camouflages it as well. To what extent are themed spaces beginning to set the agenda for public culture? Where do the crowds flock to in practically every major town in the developed world? We are indeed becoming tourists in our own life, and must turn that process into as complex a statement as the Baroque was, and see the paradoxes as honestly as possible.

1 Filippo Baldinucci, *The Life of Bernini*, tr. K. Engass (University Park: Pennsylvania State University Press, 1966), p. 40.

2 Andrea Pozzo, Church of Saint Ignazio in Rome. The Renaissance and Baroque examples run into the thousands, of course. Jon Jerde is fascinated particularly by the narrative architecture of Borromini, and by anamorphic art in the Italian Renaissance.

3 See Michael Kubovny, *The Psychology of Perspective and Renaissance Art* (Cambridge: Cambridge University Press, 1986), chapters 3, 4 and 8 in particular. Scholars in perception have remapped the shifts in pespective almost scientifically, found patterns and intentions that clearly point toward a walk-through narrative code evolving from Renaissance forms in the sixteenth century.

4 Jose Antonio Maravall, *The Culture of the Baroque: Analysis of a Historical Structure*, tr. T. Cochran (Minneapolis: University of Minnesota Press, 1986; orig. in Spanish, 1975), pp. 82ff.

5 I realize that this does not fit the Habermasian definition of the public sphere. For an earlier reading of the problem, see Thomas Crow, *Painters and Public Life in Eighteenth-Century Paris* (New Haven: Yale University Press, 1985).

6 Corporate interests can be equated with "corporate bodies" in early modern Europe: the various mercantilist, clerical and atavistic medieval institutions that made that era as much a political palimpsest as our own. The extra-national power of many of these corporate bodies also can be seen as a parallel.

7 The system of centralized control attributed to Louis XIV, though, in fact, Louis was accommodating frequently to his visitors, to the court, to parallel systems of old noblesse. Louis' pomp appeared absolutist, as a symbol of power, but underneath he was clearly in alliance with business interests, through his minister Colbert, etc. It was a kind of divine right insured through business.

8 Much of Baroque scripted space—the staging, the narrative—relies on theatrical effects from the Renaissance theater, for example, in sources translated for the anthology *The Renaissance Stage: Documents of Serlio, Sabbatini and Furttenbach*, ed. Barnard Hewitt (Coral Gables: University of Miami Press, 1958).

9 Possibly the most famous of these handbooks was written by Fra Andrea Pozzo, *Perspectiva Pictorum* (1693–98).

10 Max Weber, *The Protestant Ethic and the Spirit of Capitalism* (New York: Scribner Book Company, 1977).

11 Roland Barthes, *Mythologies*, tr. A. Lavers (New York: Hill and Wang, 1972; orig. 1957), in particular "Myth Today," p. 109ff.

12 From an interview with Jon Jerde by the author, 1998. Jerde was referring to the movie sets in Abbott and Costello movies of the 1940s, not so much the color as the cheap materials, so self-reflexive, so much a vaudeville of the referent. He could also have mentioned *Night in Casablanca*, the Marx Brothers comedy of 1946, which most fits his example. In these films, the protagonists wander through the sets like shoppers in an adventure.

Times Square, New York, New York, USA.

Giovanni Bernini, Triton Fountain, Rome, Italy.

Universal City Masterplan & Universal CityWalk The Universal City masterplan creates a pedestrian-oriented "urban village" crowning the hillside citadel of Universal film and television studios and theme park in Hollywood. Sited where the Los Angeles basin, downtown area and San Fernando Valley meet, the 1989 masterplan was designed to create a regional hub for jobs, entertainment and services. The plan reinforces the natural gradients of the site, and re-creates the image of a "city on the hill." It clusters workplace, shopping, entertainment, cultural, hotel, eating and recreation uses into low-rise districts and public plazas amid the existing studios, tour, backlot sets and adjacent residential areas. Phase One, CityWalk, constructed in 1993, forms the central spine of the Universal City masterplan.

YOU
ARE
HERE
⇩

In 1989, Lew Wasserman, then head of MCA Development (which is now Universal Creative, run by Edgar Bronfman, Jr.), commissioned the Jerde Partnership to reevaluate its hilltop attractions. Universal Studios Hollywood is the world's largest film and television studio, and the second largest tourist attraction in Southern California, drawing more than five million visitors each year to its combination of attractions—theme park, Universal Amphitheater, and 18-screen Universal City Cinemas complex. The Jerde Partnership masterplan for the 425-acre (172 ha.) site surrounds and encloses these amenities with an arrangement of concentric and radiating streets. The

"Each host city or town has a unique signature psyche. Each inhabitant has a fantasy that is either bigger or smaller than real life. Significant urban concepts will deliver on the promise of a positive fantasy in a real way."

Jon Jerde

design invokes the spirit of dense, lively neighborhoods in older cities, such as the Latin Quarter in Paris, North Beach area of San Francisco, or Soho in London. Jerde considers that the masterplan "continues the idea of city or village as icon; consciously constructed in this case, with a collection of uses whose purpose is to produce a singular product: entertainment."

The Jerde Partnership's response is also intended to encourage a sense of community in an area of uncontrolled growth. By providing all the uses and services needed by local residents, maximizing access, diversity and convenience, it can reduce car-dependency and create work for the community.

The project is designed as a "city roof," or dome, recalling the shallow disc conceived for the Satellite New Town (see p. 60). Jerde describes this disc as "cut apart by a network of walkways, roadways and nodes." In the masterplan, a central spine connects the entertainment uses on the hill.

Universal CityWalk is the constructed version of this central spine, a 1,500 foot (450 m.) long pedestrian "street" connecting the scattered elements of Universal City. Designed as a strong, safe pedestrian link between the site's three disparate existing destinations: the 6,200-seat

Above: Rendered section of the masterplan illustrating the "city roof" concept.

Opposite: Rendered site plan of Universal City.

Pages 126–27: Aerial view of CityWalk.

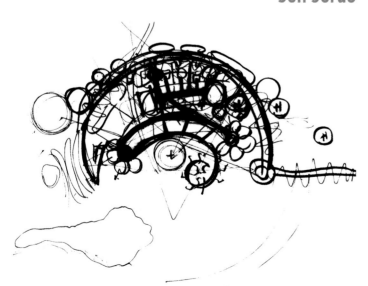

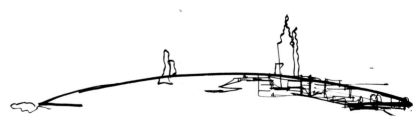

Left: Conceptual sketch of Universal City Masterplan.

Right: Sketch of "city roof" concept for masterplan.

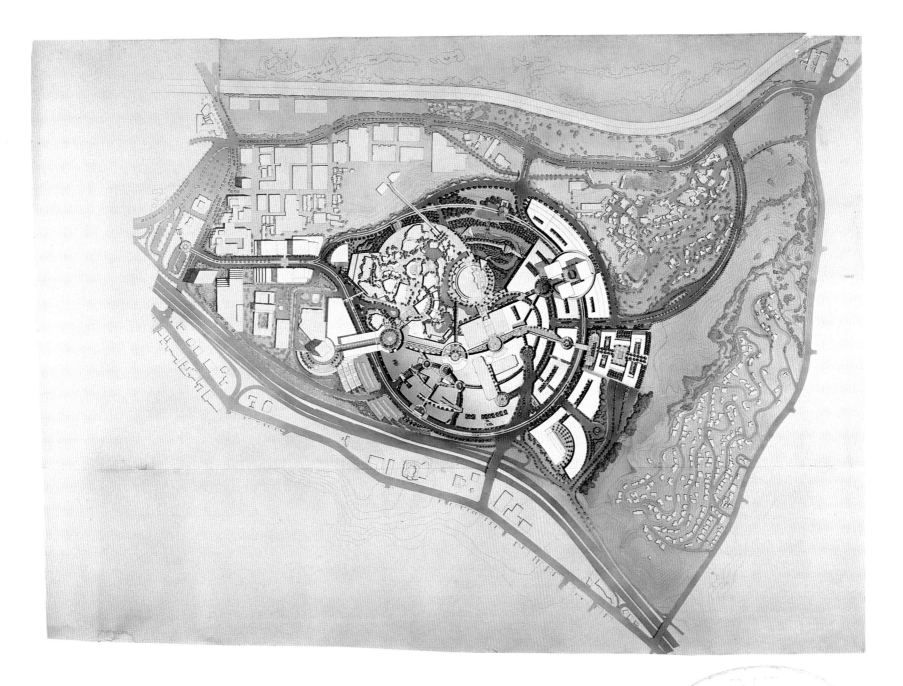

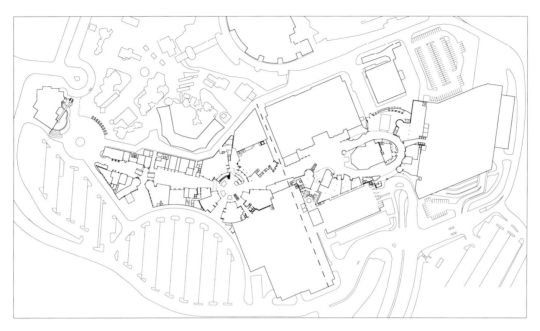

Left: Site plan of Phases One and Two, showing CityWalk.

Below: Section showing facades on CityWalk.

amphitheater, 18-screen cinema, theme park and tour, CityWalk is both unique and familiar—a collage of the images and characteristics of vernacular Los Angeles architecture. The project's buildings are formulated from a "kit of parts" of generic components: decorative tower and marquee elements, flat simple facades with a layering of various grids and signage. The street is further layered with CityWalk's neon signs and images. With its bevy of playful buildings, each colored and sign-posted, CityWalk is a mosaic of small, anonymous buildings (not Los Angeles icons), exaggerated and compressed into a pedestrian-scaled terrace of buildings.

CityWalk has two streets, EastWalk and WestWalk, containing shops, restaurants, nightclubs, bars, theaters and a college, that meet at Fountain Court. This open, circular courtyard covered by a steel-framed dome, with walls sheathed in pregrown "landscape panels," draws crowds to its street performers and central water feature.

To instill an authentic street quality, the firm used a co-creative process, collaborating in this instance with the tenants. Instead of setting finite standards for storefronts, signage, and lighting, the Jerde Partnership has encouraged individual innovative, distinctive tenant designs, intended to demonstrate pride of ownership and to help create a textured street, full of life and perpetual change.

CityWalk Phase Two is now being designed by the Jerde Partnership and is due to be completed in 2000.

Top right: CityWalk's pedestrian scale and open ambiance encourage movement through shops and venues, as seen looking east along WestWalk.

Left: CityWalk, Phase One of the larger Universal City Masterplan, is designed to distill the quality of Los Angeles street life into an area three blocks long.

Below left: The signage framework doubles as a grid that contains theatrical lighting, creating an outdoor nightclub setting.

Below right: The water feature provides an interesting diversion along CityWalk. Fountain designed by WET Design.

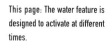

Opposite: View into Fountain Court.

Below: One of CityWalk's three outdoor plazas.

Right: CityWalk's building facades, such as this 75 foot (22 meter) neon sign, have an accentuated scale and serve as district landmarks.

Pages 134—35: Street scene of CityWalk.

The Fremont Street Experience is a linear, urban canopy of light, music and sound that reactivates Las Vegas' iconic "Glitter Gulch," by transforming five city blocks into a covered, pedestrian-only destination. This project, completed in 1995, is an example of urban spectacle, in which existing neon-covered casino facades, and the sky and ground planes are fashioned into a "tube of light."

Opposite: The entrance to the
"tube of light."

Left: Fremont Street "before."

"Our stuff isn't supposed to be visual.
It's supposed to be visceral." Jon Jerde

The invention of neon transformed Las Vegas in the 1940s. Fremont Street, with its casino signage fueled by electricity from the nearby Boulder Dam, was quickly dubbed "Glitter Gulch." Known for famous signs such as Vegas Vic and Vegas Vickie, it became the historic heart of Nevada's gaming industry, and is Las Vegas' most iconic image.

By the early 1990s, however, the casinos on Fremont Street had suffered a serious decline in revenue as they were eclipsed by mega-resorts on the Las Vegas Strip. In 1992, the concerned owners of downtown's casinos and hotels joined with the City of Las Vegas to improve the public perception of downtown and to bring back its audience. A consortium lead by colorful casino mogul Steve Wynn, for whom the Jerde Partnership designed Buccaneer Bay at Treasure Island and, more recently, Bellagio, asked the Jerde Partnership for a solution.

The group had already considered various ideas, including turning Fremont Street into a Venice-style canal. But one night after visiting the dilapidated Fremont Street Jerde, seeing the brilliantly lit facades against dark sky and street, had a vision of a "tube of light," in which these dark planes would also be illuminated. Fremont Street represented a generic grouping of resort casinos that was extremely compact, in total contrast to the wide spaces of the Strip. This compactness was to be exploited at Fremont Street. All of the casino hotels could be packaged into one colossal complex: the largest casino in the world. Effectively, the Fremont Street Experience would turn the street into an outside room, a grand lobby for the individual casino hotels that kept their original facades.

The Fremont Street Experience uses light to create a new sensory experience for downtown Las Vegas. The existing street was turned into one giant outdoor room, 2,000 feet (600 m.) long, 100 feet (30 m.) wide and 100 feet (30 m.) high. This was accomplished by eliminating vehicular traffic, unifying the pedestrian floor, and creating a soaring barrel vault. This "celestial vault," covered with 2.1 million lights, comes alive nightly at dusk, on the hour, with a "Light Spectacular," designed by Jeremy Railton. This digitized light display is accompanied by symphonic sound booming out of a 540,000-watt sound system.

The project has spawned a significant amount of new investment and revitalization in downtown Las Vegas. More than 25 million people visited this spectacular Las Vegas attraction within the first three years of its completion. "Five years ago, we couldn't find anyone to invest a dollar in downtown Las Vegas," said Mayor Jan Laverty Jones in 1996, "today, that's changed."

YOU
ARE
HERE
⇩

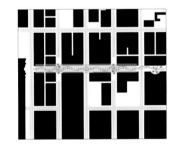

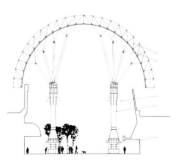

Above: Section through the tube.

Far left: Rendered conceptual
sketch, by Jerde, of "sky parade."

Left: The Fremont Street
Experience as constructed.

This page and opposite: Views of
the Fremont Street Experience by
night and day.

Opposite: The original neon signs gave Las Vegas its glamorous reputation.

This page: Different stages of the Light Spectacular designed by Jeremy Railton.

Pages 144–45: The lightweight canopy creates a shared "lobby" for the hotel casinos along the Fremont Street Experience. Each has kept its original facade.

Santa Fe Town Center The Jerde Partnership's unbuilt 1995 design for a 2,100-acre regional masterplan for Santa Fe, a new district of Mexico City, includes office space and broadcast facilities for media companies, a new university and housing of a broad range of densities. The town center, with hotel, office, residential, recreational and cultural uses, is linked to a pedestrian-oriented base of restaurants, nightclubs and specialty retail comprising 323,000 square feet.

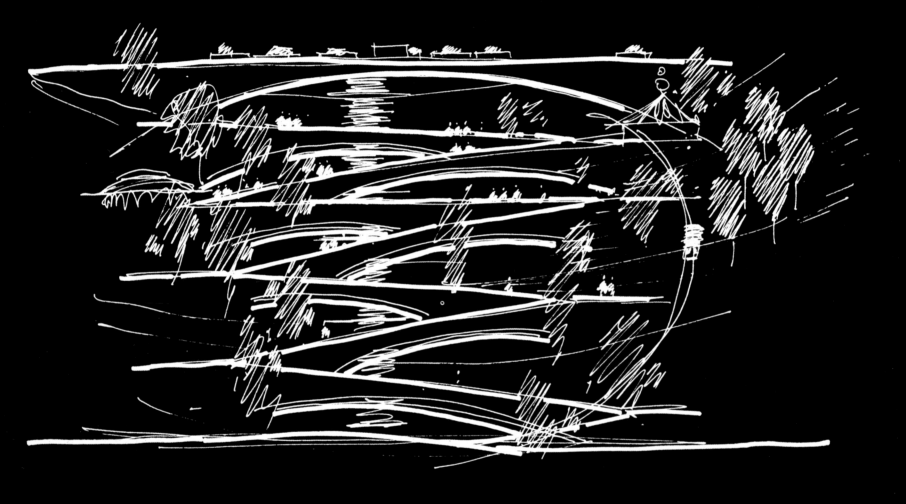

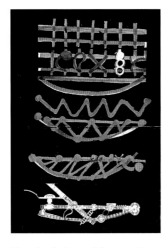

Opposite: The site's lower and upper regions are connected by a grand staircase, similar to the Spanish Steps in Rome.

Left: Concept sketch.

Far right: Sketch diagram of plan.

YOU
ARE
HERE
⇩

The site is located in an old gravel quarry. Its widely varying topography is defined by a freeway on one side and a deep valley on the other, and the project area winds along the ridge of a steeply sloping site. The plan combines sites in the lower and upper regions. An upper park engages with a park in the town center that Jerde believes "will create a flowing continuity of place where communal activities can occur." This sloping park is a landscaped canyon, the edges of which contain stepped courtyard housing, anchored by a retail entertainment complex.

A grand staircase forms the connection between the lower and upper parks. Offices and housing are distributed along a serpentine boulevard that winds through the site. Further connecting the upper and lower areas is an iconic bar-shaped building, containing retail and entertainment, that functions as a bridge and defines the town center. An ascending axial street runs beside the building, terminating at the conference center and showcase communications complex that anchor the upper zone.

To synthesize the Indian (Aztec/Mayan) and European (Spanish) history of the site, the firm collaborated on this project with Los Angeles-based, Mexican-American artist Robert Graham. The project uses ornately carved local stone of varied textures to give a regional identity.

Right: Watercolor painting of plan by Jon Jerde.

Below: Sketch plan depicting the bar-shaped building and serpentine boulevard that winds through the site.

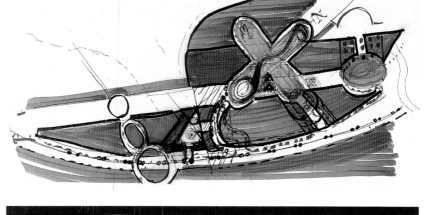

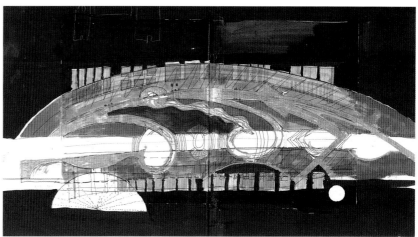

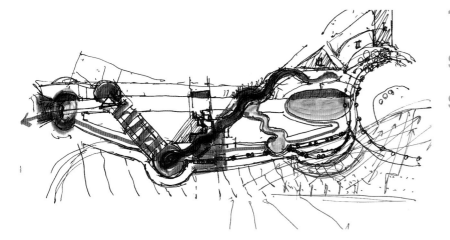

"Modernist design used humans as background scenery. Experiential design is background scenery for humans." Jon Jerde

Robina Town Centre is located on the Australian Gold Coast at the southern terminus of the Brisbane–Gold Coast railway line, in an area experiencing rapid population growth. As the center of an 86-acre development completed in 1996, Robina integrates shopping, entertainment, office and community functions into a villagelike core. Sited at the edge of a lake on a sloping site with mountain and coastal views, the Robina design recreates an Italian hill town, with pedestrian streets, plazas and galleria connected by a terraced armature.

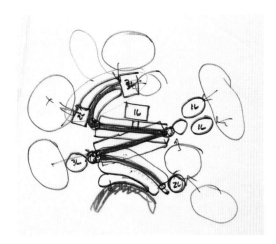

Left: Sketch diagram showing the terraced circulation armature.

YOU ARE HERE ⇩

Robina Town Centre is a new 1.3 million square foot (125,000 s.m.) regional development for the fast-growing suburban community of Robina. The Jerde Partnership takes advantage of the site's 60 foot (20 m.) gradient to the lake to provide a terraced circulation armature that connects retail and entertainment uses and offers vistas across the water. Branching off the armature are breezeways, formed by trellis and tented structures that shade and protect from the elements. Towers along the armature are used as orientation devices and to create a distinctive skyline.

The program combines an innovative mix of com-

"We create colonies of cohesion." Jon Jerde

mercial activity that ranges from discount retail stores to boutique and specialty stores. This mix of retail in the district evokes marketplace typologies throughout the world (bazaars, high street). At the top of the hill a convenience-oriented discount center serves immediate needs. Luxury, market rate, discount and value-related districts make up the middle of the project. At the bottom an entertainment and attraction zone relates directly to the lakefront.

Robina was designed to reflect the vernacular of the area, providing a variation on Queensland's tropical architecture, using a palette of textured concrete block, metal roofs and lime-washed walls.

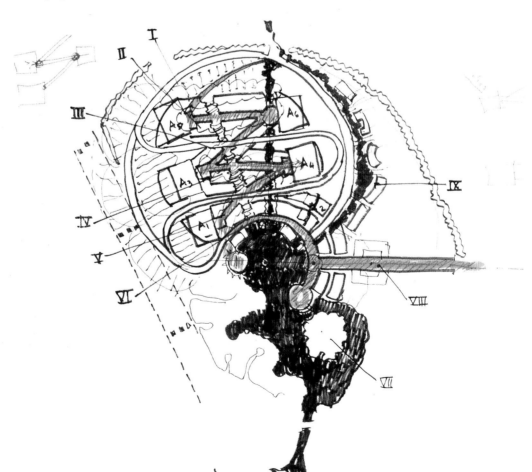

Left: Sketch diagram of site plan, with armature, various commercial elements and lake.

Below: Rendered section through
development.

Bottom: Rendered section.

Opposite, left: View of the lake-front facade.

Opposite, below: View from above, of plazas along the terraced circulation armature.

This page: Landscaping and water features along the armature create open spaces and enclosure.

Beursplein is a large-scale, multiuse urban development in the center of Rotterdam. The insertion of an armature, completed in 1996, in the form of a below-grade pedestrian concourse, has connected existing but distinct shopping and market districts on either side of the city's main thoroughfare, known as the Coolsingel, and improved the area around the busy Beursplein Metro Station. Set below the city, yet open to the sky under a sinuous glass canopy, the concourse is accessible by ramps and stairs, escalators and elevators.

Left: Section through concourse.

Opposite: View of access to the underground concourse.

YOU
ARE
HERE
⇩

Rotterdam suffered intense, targeted bombing during World War II, fracturing its urban fabric. Rotterdam's Lijnbaan shopping district, adjacent to the Beursplein, was planned during the reconstruction of the city after the war. As the first pedestrian-only street in Europe, the shopping district was human-scaled, in a linear grid of one- and two-story shops. The landmark Bijenkorf department store designed by Marcel Breuer is here, and other distinguished department stores anchor the nearby Beursplein and Van Oldenbarneveld plazas.

Designed in a utilitarian, Modernist style, Lijnbaan was never entirely successful. When residential growth expanded into Rotterdam's suburbs in the 1970s, retail and other amenities moved away from the urban core and the site suffered as a result. In addition, the city's widest thoroughfare, the Coolsingel, divided Lijnbaan from the Beursplein/Hoogstraat retail and market area, seriously disrupting the functions of the inner city. Effectively, the vehicular intrusion sliced the city in half. The congestion further intensified in 1996 when the area became the primary access to the city center across the new Erasmus Bridge.

Dutch developer Multi Vastgoed b.v. asked the Jerde Partnership to address both the ailing urban core and the congestion. The firm, in collaboration with Dutch architects T&T Design and De Architekten cie, removed the Coolsingel barrier by laying down an urban armature, or spine, a new shopping street—Beursplein Promenade— that passes under this major thoroughfare that connects to the busy Beursplein Metro Station. Described by Jerde as a "large-scale urban accessory," this new 1,000-foot (300 m.) street, a sinuous reversing curve, connects ground-level plazas on either side of the Coolsingel.

Beursplein Promenade is inspired by the juxtaposition of old (prewar) and new city. Heavy stone walls had protected the old city; straight, orthogonal street grids, steel and glass defined postwar building. Therefore, one side of Beursplein Promenade is lined with shops framed with natural stone portals and planters, the other with storefronts that glitter in metal and glass. Beursplein has a subtle palette of greys, of stone, silvery glass and metal. The Promenade is covered by a curved, ornamental glass canopy, which shelters pedestrians from the weather. Other elements on the site include a three-level shopping gallery, the lower level of which connects to Beursplein Promenade. Other elements of the project also involved the renovation and expansion of the Beurs Metro Station, which serves 70,000 passengers daily, together with the Bulgersteyn, a 30-floor residential tower.

Right: Plan.

"The challenge of the new millennium is to put things back together that once were whole."
Jon Jerde

This page: The curved
ornamental canopy runs the
length of the promenade.
The shops on one side of the
promenade are faced with
natural stone portals, while on
the other side, the frontages
are constructed of metal and
glass.

Opposite: The canopy glows in
the dark.

160

Canal City Hakata is one of the largest privately developed real-estate projects in Japan's history. A mixed-use district woven into the urban fabric of Fukuoka, it is a synergistic mix of East-meets-West, a hybrid of local and global identities, built environment and natural landscape. Completed in 1996, Canal City Hakata uses the Japanese aesthetic principle *wa* (harmony) to integrate disparate elements, seeking neither to conquer the new and exotic nor to mirror the cultural traditions and history of Japan.

Right: Conceptual diagram showing
districts, with text describing the
"experiential" qualities of each.

Below right: Early conceptual
sketch plan showing the canal
armature and its connection to the
Naka River.

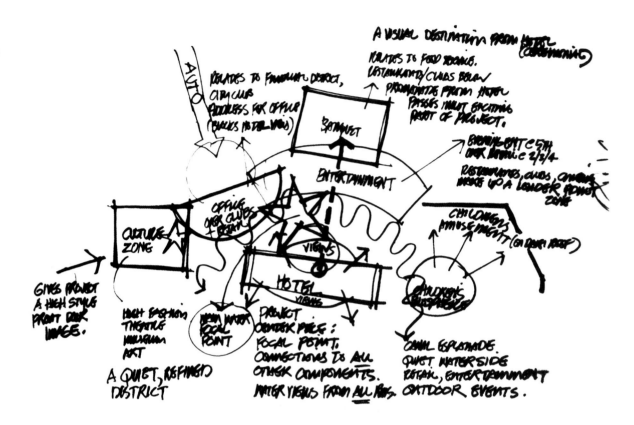

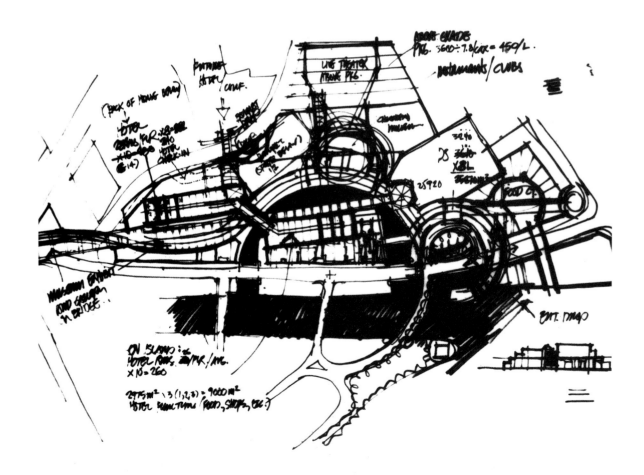

YOU
ARE
HERE
⇩

The 2.5 million square foot (240,000 s.m.) mixed-use complex Canal City Hakata features a number of buildings dispersed along a new canal. Incorporated into the Western program of hotel, office and commercial uses are places that express the individual spirit of the locale; areas for festive events, spontaneous markets, performances and community meetings. Canal City Hakata evolved from a cultural collaboration; the Japanese client, their California-based architect, and a mix of local and international tenants.

Each decade, a Japanese ministry pronounces an economic and industrial vision for the country. In the 1990s, in response to the stresses of urbanization and over-industriousness, that vision has been "honor the common man." Simultaneously, the expanded economic growth that pushed Japan into the global arena as a world leader called for the internationalization of several provincial cities, including Fukuoka. Historically, Fukuoka has been at the crossroads between trade, ideas and exchanges in Asia. Cultures and religions of early Chinese and European civilizations were first introduced there, then spread to the rest of Japan. Its openness is reflected in the ideas and values of the clients, whose mission was "to create entirely new concepts in urban development."

The design process began with the premise that the design should not impose a Western model on a foreign culture—as, for example, Le Corbusier did at Chandigarh in India—but rather it would both inform and be informed by its cultural condition. In the words of the firm, Canal City Hakata merges tradition and modernity, East and West in a brew so well mixed that it is hard to identify distinctly opposing elements. Such fusion can be seen in the contrasting color palettes—the normally subdued and natural colors of Japanese daily life and traditional arts are combined with explosive American festival hues and the use of bold color at a large scale rather than as accent. The project also uses nature as a unifying metaphor, as

"Great cities become so by the many layers of anonymous editing over time. The challenge in the design of large scale, short time-frame places is to allow a guided sequential layering of individuals and institutions to inform the final collage." Jon Jerde

Above: Aerial view showing the project's internal armature, a canal. A hotel, cineplex, amusement center, and business center all surround the 'negative sphere' at Sun Plaza, the project's main gathering place.

Below: Longitudinal section through the five zones of Canal City Hakata.

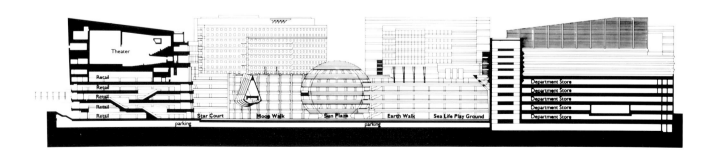

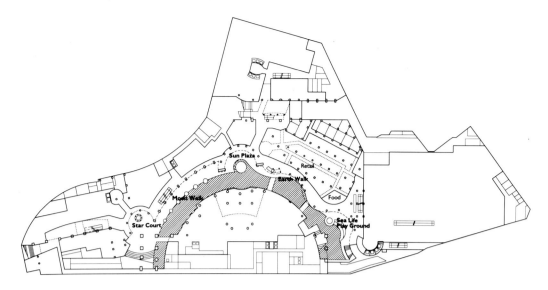

expressed in the canal, the canyonlike buildings and the allusions to the cosmos in the five districts that make up the complex.

Canal City Hakata is located on a 9-acre site that was vacated by a large apparel manufacturer. The project's organizing spatial element is a new canal, inspired by the site's proximity to the Naka River. Buildings rise from either side of the canal. Their bases are stone with horizontal banding, like layers of strata, a reference to the erosion of land as a river passes through a canyon over centuries. As the buildings ascend, their materials become more modern, refined and lighter. The canal edges vary, from hard-edged, where water meets a "cliff" face, to softer, at the fringes of meandering streams. Paving materials are geologic, with patterns of sand, stone and mineral deposits, inset with fossils and shells.

There are four anchors in the project: Fukuoka City Theater, Daiei's Mega Vandle value-based department store and supermarket, the Grand Hyatt Hotel, and Canal City Business Center. The centerpiece 425-room Grand Hyatt Hotel connects to retail and entertainment uses across the canal by a pedestrian network. The project also has a secondary organization oriented around five districts. Continuing the theme of nature, these five zones are

each named for a part of the universe: Star Court, Moon Walk, Sun Plaza, Earth Walk, and Sea Court. The project's centerpiece is a ceremonial "negative sphere" representing the sun. Each district is identified by a "wayfinding," or orientation sculpture standing 40 feet (12 m.) above the project's central canal. Four fountains also blend spiritual, mythological and historic icons.

Landscaping along the planted canal and its five districts is a unifying element. Trees surrounding Canal City Hakata's exterior extend the shaded pedestrian environment to nearby streets, providing a human-scaled canopy, and creating a landscaped edge for new buildings and a framework for future enhancement of the surrounding areas.

Canal City has regenerated its neighborhood and reversed decline in the previously dying historic shopping arcade Kamikawabata, through whose alleys Canal City's many visitors must traverse. Cited by Japanese architect Arata Isozaki as one of the most important architectural projects of 1996, Canal City, with its synergistic blend of Fukuoka, Asia, and the West, brings global viability to a place that desires to become one of the world's great modern cities. It also serves as a twenty-first-century model for large-scale, multiuse private developments.

Above: Ground level plan.

Opposite: A pedestrian bridge links the subway system and existing shopping districts to Canal City Hakata's north entrance.

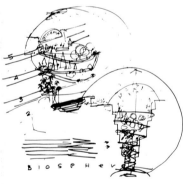

Above: Conceptual sketch of the Sun Plaza, drawn by Jon Jerde.

Right: Painting by Jon Jerde.

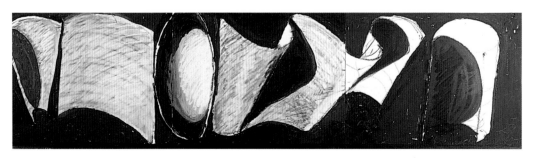

Opposite: Several pedestrian
bridges connect Sun Plaza to a
luxury hotel.

Below left: The Moon Walk at
canal level connects the Star
Court and Sun Plaza.

Below center: "Wayfinding"
sculptures help to orient visitors
in each district.

Below right: Looking north
towards the chapel (upper left).

Opposite: Looking north into Canal City Hakata, to the Sun Plaza amphitheater, and the "wiggle wall" fronting a cinema complex and high-tech amusement center.

Left: Canal City Hakata's five districts are connected by an interior canal.

Below left: Sun Plaza from above.

Below: Looking into the terraces of Sun Plaza during a performance.

Bottom right: Star Court from above.

East-facing interior facade with
Sun Plaza to the center.

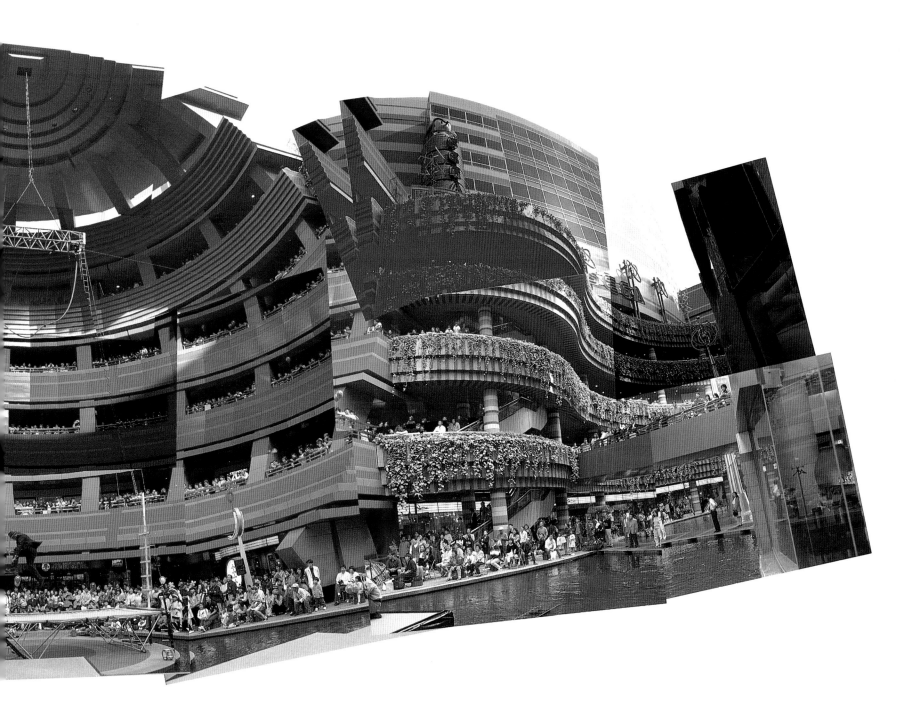

Bellagio The Jerde Partnership, commissioned by Steve Wynn of Mirage Resorts to design "simply the world's finest hotel" and resort casino, has designed the $1.9 billion Bellagio, which opened in October 1998. The project surrounds an eleven-acre, manmade lake on the former site of the legendary Dunes Hotel on the Strip in Las Vegas, and has 4 million square feet of built area, landscaped gardens and an arcaded conservatory on a 126-acre site. The exterior is modeled on Italianate lakefront villas.

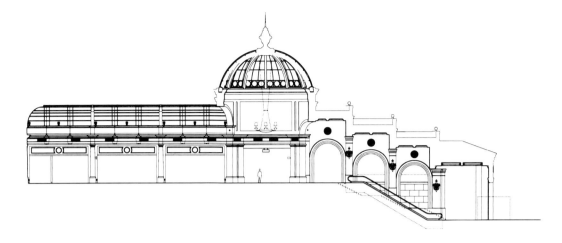

YOU
ARE
HERE
⇩

The Las Vegas Strip is an endless string of ever-more fantastical casinos, each one a re-creation of an urban condition, myth or monument from world history (the Luxor, New York New York, Treasure Island). Bellagio takes this typology to another level. At Bellagio, the Jerde Partnership introduced European urban design strategies to create pedestrian-oriented public spaces in place of the private, enclosed places typical of other casinos. Bellagio provides Las Vegas with new urban experiences: window-shopping in a bustling arcade, dining in open-air cafes, visiting a museum. Bellagio's tree-lined sidewalks fronting the lake, its glass-covered shopping arcade, and garden conservatory are designed for the public realm.

The Jerde Partnership developed the site plan of the project, which is modeled on the villages surrounding Lake Como, and designed the exteriors and some of the interior spaces, including the conservatory, retail promenade, registration courtyard and pool area. (Wynn's in-house design firm, Atlandia Design, was responsible for the rest, including the 36-story hotel tower).

The conservatory is an arcaded interior garden that connects the western arm of the resort to the lobby. It is lined with dining areas and an art gallery, which houses Steve Wynn's $300 million collection of Impressionist,

Modern and Contemporary paintings and sculpture. Styled on historic European arcades, the retail promenade has 50-foot (15 m.) high domed rotundas with carved plaster ceilings and glass skylights, and richly detailed storefronts. The luxury retail spaces have been leased to Giorgio Armani, Gucci, Chanel, Prada, Hermès and Tiffany.

The hotel contains 3,000 guest rooms, and nine villas scattered throughout the site are 6,000 square feet (560 s.m.) each. Bellagio also has two wedding chapels, reception and health facilities, including a spa and several outdoor pools. A multiphased monorail system is being constructed to transport guests to and from Bellagio, Monte Carlo and The Mirage casinos.

Far left: Site plan, showing lake and surrounding buildings.

Above: Section.

Below: Watercolor rendering of the Italianate village exterior modeled on those found at Lake Como in Italy.

Opposite: Lakefront village along exterior facade.

Pages 178–79: Exterior facade.

"We are like psychoanalysts, uncovering the dreams of our clients and helping to make them come true." Jon Jerde

Right: Entrance to retail armature from the Strip.

Opposite: Interior of retail armature.

Left: Photomontage.

Opposite and below left: Garden conservatory with the Bellagio Gallery of Art (left).

Far Left: Views of the luxury retail promenade.

Below: Porte-cochere.

Left: The fountain at Bellagio.

Above: Poolside area.

Bellagio, Las Vegas, Nevada, USA

A Bellagio terrace facing the lake
and new casino construction
across the street.

And, Tomorrow ... the World? Craig Hodgetts

Many would argue that the work in this volume is not architecture. They would suggest that this work lacks the inner consistency, the harmony, and the discipline required to merit close study. And they would dismiss its obvious commercial success as one more example of a culture gone wrong.

Among many architects, Jon Jerde's impulse to embrace the vagaries of superstores and food courts is as inexplicable, and nearly as offensive, as the impulse to deface a beloved monument. Then there are the others—poets and novelists, the followers of Jane Jacobs and Mike Davis, who hold that only evolving communities can create urban vitality, and that those created by the will of a single designer are doomed to a sterile existence and lingering obsolescence.

Jon Jerde is one of that breed of innovators whose contagious vision redefines not only an era, but so shapes the boundaries of conventional architectural practice that new disciplines must be invented in order to realize the possibilities. Architecture may be his medium, one could argue, but not his message.

And he has done it with shopping.

Not just any shopping, but shopping that treats the consumer as audience. An audience to be seduced, teased, and fulfilled. His architectural framework, far from locking visitors into a singular, "aesthetically unified" experience, suggests multiple, individually defined scenarios which, in their variety and incongruity, emulate those of a "found" environment. His brash synthesis of quasi-urban spaces represents a new way of **experiencing architecture**, rather than simply seeing it. His designs would, quite frankly, be unthinkable in a world without television, modems, global brands and the appetites they have created.

Let's face it, the instinct to shop has not risen to the top of the culture charts. Ubiquitous, and taken for granted as the fuel for more elevated pursuits, the typical architectural rejoinder to consumer cravings

has been to provide a quiet, useful background for the mountains of goods which usher in each season.

But today, with catalogues, discount centers and the pervasive eradication of place brought about by a co-conspiracy of ATMs, In 'n Out's, gated communities and strip developments, the old-fashioned shopping center has emerged as … *voilà* … a proto-town center, and Jon Jerde has been there to shepherd its evolution.

A glance at the marauding curves filling his sketchbooks reveals a flagrant, utopian, imagination, full of ideas that seem simultaneously improbable and necessary. Ideas that convey an impetuous world-view that seems at odds with the big-time developers and power-brokers that hustle to build his projects around the world. Is it obvious to them that these sketches are blueprints for far-reaching, radical and profoundly democratic ideas about the way people might gather in the next millennium?

These are places shorn of false hierarchy, whose formal incongruities generate a hodge-podge sponge of opportunities which would challenge the most creative leasing agent, yet which, once occupied, would seem to have the assurance of a long-established district. One's first impression, that the welter of materials and forms has evolved naturally, replete with remodelings, failed one-offs, and pastiche overlays, affirms Jerde's skill at portraying the impressions called forth by famously accretive cities like **Rome**, whose fabled evolution from Imperial City to barbaric encampment to Papal Seat can be traced from every stone. Jerde's romance with Rome, and his fascination with the scarred skin of a city that has seen it all, suggests that his conceptual demands reach far beyond bricks and mortar to the creation of a back story—a prequel. This prequel helps to embed its structure in a fictional context to which the final design must adapt, creating a palimpsest much like that found in Rome.

In fact, the debut of Jerde's vision didn't exist in conventional space-time at all, but instead was seen on television by the worldwide audience of the 1984 Olympics (coincidentally, not long after Frank Gehry completed his now-famous house in Santa Monica, and Michael Graves was being initiated as the crown prince of the then emerging kingdom of the post-modern). Never mind that the majority of the structures were temporary, and that many of the more striking images were created by Jerde's co-creators: under Jerde's leadership, the design elements for the Olympics focused on the story that could be told by the television camera, rather than the immediate experience of the audience, with results which accurately presage the actively cinematic architecture of his present work.

There is an old adage in film-making—that no one will care about your movie if they don't care about your characters. Thus, as Jerde's *leitmotif* elevates the tenant from bit player to star, that search for "just the right tenant" is often as fragile and creative as casting, with many of the same caveats. Nevertheless, even though Jerde's idea—that architecture might help to launch and shape the businesses it is designed to shelter—might seem obvious in hindsight, it stands in sharp contrast to the traditional developer's role of leasing generic space.

Why hasn't this been done before? Malls, it turns out, have a historic grip on the rejuvenation of urban centers, starting with the obvious ones, like that of the **Galleria** in Milan, or the **Burlington Arcade** in London, but even here in the United States, with notable examples in Cleveland and St. Louis. Jerde's twentieth-century versions start with an obvious premise—if a concentration of retail experience is able to become the reference point for outlying areas, as Joyce Carol Oates, Douglas Coupland, and others have described, and does so with no particular architectural distinction (one thinks of *Fast Times at Ridgemont High*, and the utter bewilderment of teens with no other place to go), then is it not obvious that the experience itself is fundamental to the societal construct, yet it is so basic that it begs for elaboration.

The creation of **the shopping center in the 1950s**, when urban flight was eviscerating city centers, was most certainly also predicated on a mix of racism, naïveté, and misplaced utopian impulses, yet each in its way conferred a new identity on the suburb, and continues to evolve to fulfill that need. Functional, pragmatic, a stepchild of form-follows-function wanna-bes (Victor Gruen's illustrations of a tidy, Swiss-watch of a town center come to mind) those efforts had all the excitement of a good emetic with none of the benefits, leaving the core of many cities not only barren, but constipated. The formulaic suburban shopping center—anchors at either end, small shops between, all floating in a broth of parking—was viable in the short term, but began to founder in the 1980s, when boutiques and a renewed urban consciousness recalibrated the equation.

Jerde, working in the commercial practice of Charles Kober, must have seen the train coming. Mesmerized by the shops and plazas of European cities, and inspired by the notion of townscape, he was able to challenge the conventional wisdom of the development community with the creation of Horton Plaza. In one stroke, he redefined what had been a prosaic functional diagram into an environment full of intriguing options, freeing the facades of tenants from the straitjacket of architectural conformity; empowering visitors to wander, get lost, and just discover something; and suggesting, even crafting, an intimate joinery with the surrounding city.

Not surprisingly, architects and clients trained to recognize unity as a preemptive gauge of social class, sometimes find the willful creation of such a broad spectrum of typologies offensive. After all, they have been taught that one of life's goals is to affirm status by limiting the options of the less fortunate—while Jerde seems to take genuine pleasure in offering enough options to overwhelm even Everyman. One thinks of the early "spectacular" Hollywood films, with their slumming socialites and stilted parodies of the King's English as an apt metaphor for the canonical architecture of today's world, which finds itself unable to appreciate the value of an evolving streetscape; much less capable of emulating the incremental growth of that streetscape, and finally packaging it so as to **stimulate shoppers to a near frenzy of consumption**.

Even a devoted fan (I am one) would conclude that there's not much room here for "serious" architecture, given the orgy of materials, graphic devices, odd structural interventions, and geometric carnage that form a habitual cadence in Jerde's vocabulary. Without a consistent theoretical framework, he is the ultimate outsider. Neither content to dredge up a consistent period decorum, nor to indulge in dramatic form-giving for its own sake, he has found a way to resist the anomie of a more traditional "Modernist" approach to form, and invest his projects with a rare combination of event and occasion conjured by his fantasy. He oscillates with ease between the genial science-fiction of Ray Bradbury, the cosmic archaeology of **Giovanni Piranesi**, and the high-roller energy of Frank Sinatra.

Architecture is perhaps the final frontier in the cascade of change that has dominated twentieth-century life. Inherently slow to react, the pace of architectural design has been primarily defined by cautious evolution, providing much-needed inertia to a fast-spinning world. Yet in the twentieth century, the velocity so admired by the Futurists has come to exist not only in transport and fashion, but business and finance. A new architecture must be one able to participate in the act of becoming, rather than waiting politely in the wings. Utopian dreams rarely leave the paper they are drawn upon, much less fill up daily with hundreds of thousands of people eager to explore, interact and fantasize with what Jon describes as a contemporary piazza.

Unfortunately, the conventional mechanisms of city-building, encumbered with the political and social vagaries of full-spectrum dysfunctionality, are no match for the dedicated entrepreneur who sees opportunity in the morass of urban decline. In fact, one could argue that those mechanisms are and have always been the wrong tool for the job.

But Jerde's city-building gadget may not be made of all the right stuff either. For, while his developments have shown an unabashed affinity for capital, there is little evidence that the sponsors of projects like Canal City would stretch their vision to include market-rate housing, or even more onerous urban components like jails, rehabilitation clinics or "mom and pop" stores. It is a "why not" deeply embedded in the culture of development and urban DNA that rejects the process, but will gladly tout the product. And it is difficult to imagine that anything close to Jerde's exuberance, swashbuckling geometry and fashionable carnality could be found under the counter at any but the most liberated planning agencies.

Thus the legacy of the urban inventions to be found in this volume will be found in the future rather than the present. Implanted within the mollusk-armor of inner cities, and surrounded by the confused culture of greed, neglect, necessity and hope that drives the destiny of all cities, Jerde's artificial cosmos may, in time, attain the dignity of the truly cosmopolitan—becoming, with the scars and patina of age, a place that lives in the collective unconscious. The place each of us is drawn to, and that we seek out as tourists and residents alike.

The historical center.

Children playing computer games in a store in Tokyo, Japan.

Giovanni Piranesi, *Two Roman Roads Flanked by Colossal Funerary Monuments*, etching.

Victor Gruen, Randhurst Mall, Des Plains, Illinois.

The Gateway is a 26-acre, mixed-use district sited on Union Pacific's abandoned railroad yards in Salt Lake City near the Union Pacific Railroad's "Golden Spike," the iconic point of connection between the East and West Coasts of the United States. With connection as its concept, the district is designed to create urban infill between the downtown area and the site. Due for completion in 2002, the project anticipates the arrival of the 2002 Winter Olympics by reinvigorating an under-utilized industrial site, and reinforcing the city's image.

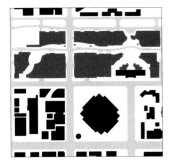

The Gateway has a mix of retail, office, hotel, cultural and entertainment uses, planned like a Western town of the 1940s, with freestanding, one- and two-story structures constructed of the local brick and concrete materials used throughout Salt Lake City.

The only existing building on the site, the historic Union Pacific depot, will serve as the project's entrance. The existing murals and stained glass inside the depot will be preserved, and the rail terminal will be restored as a public hall. The depot will open onto an open-air plaza surrounded by restaurants, cafes and small hotels. To the east of the plaza is housing, and a car-accessible, internal street connects the plaza to the project's west side, an area specifically devoted to nightlife and entertainment. A creek running through the project is modeled on one that existed previously on the site.

"The design process embodies the same pluralism that exists in cities, with accidents and surprises contributing to the complexity of the final work." Jon Jerde

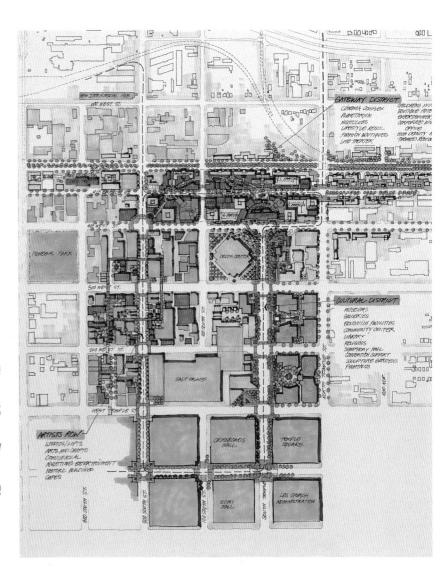

Above: Rendered site plan.

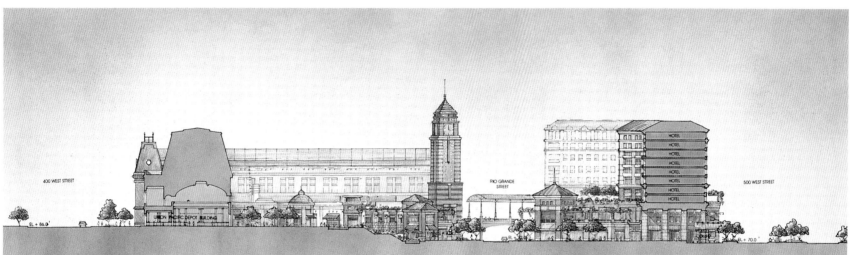

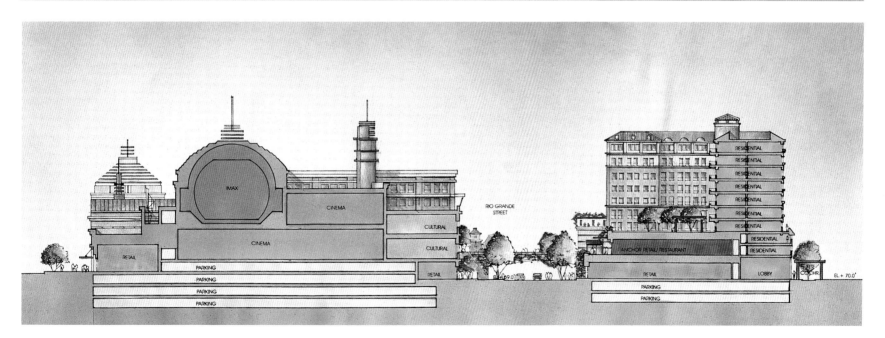

Top: Rendered elevation showing
the restored Union Pacific depot.

Center: Rendered section.

Bottom: Rendered section
through entertainment complex.

One Reeperbahn is a 322,000 square foot, mixed-use, entertainment-oriented project on the corner of one of the liveliest streets in Hamburg's St. Pauli district. The project, a series of totemlike towers that ring the edges of a grand sunken plaza, will transform the "sinful mile" of the Reeperbahn, once devoted solely to adult entertainment, into a district with a wide range of amenities for family-oriented visitors when it opens in 2001.

Below left: Local materials, especially those with a varied texture, will be used.

Below: Diagrammatic site plan.

One Reeperbahn's concept responds to the dynamic between the historic walled medieval city, of which the former gateway serves as the project site, and the untamed landscape beyond. The new building's exterior facade is flattened and fragmented into oblique angles. The walls are broken down and the city enters into the project—just as the walls of the medieval city were breached.

The project design stands the typical retail "dumbbell" plan vertically, arranging anchor tenants and stores in towers reminiscent of a nearby fortress. The towers provide prominence to the project at the street edge. Anchors on the lowest level (two levels below grade) and the top level emphasize the vertical movement in the project. The cinemas (including an IMAX theater) stack downwards from the top. A hotel is included in the facilities provided for retail and entertainment.

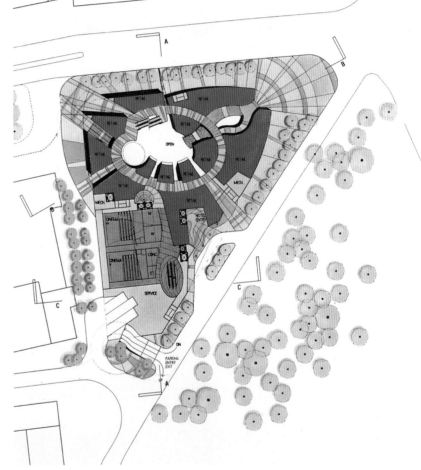

"Our curves are not formal, but perceptual; they are used to draw people in." Jon Jerde

Left: Model.

Opposite: Conceptual collages depicting "experiential" aspects of the project.

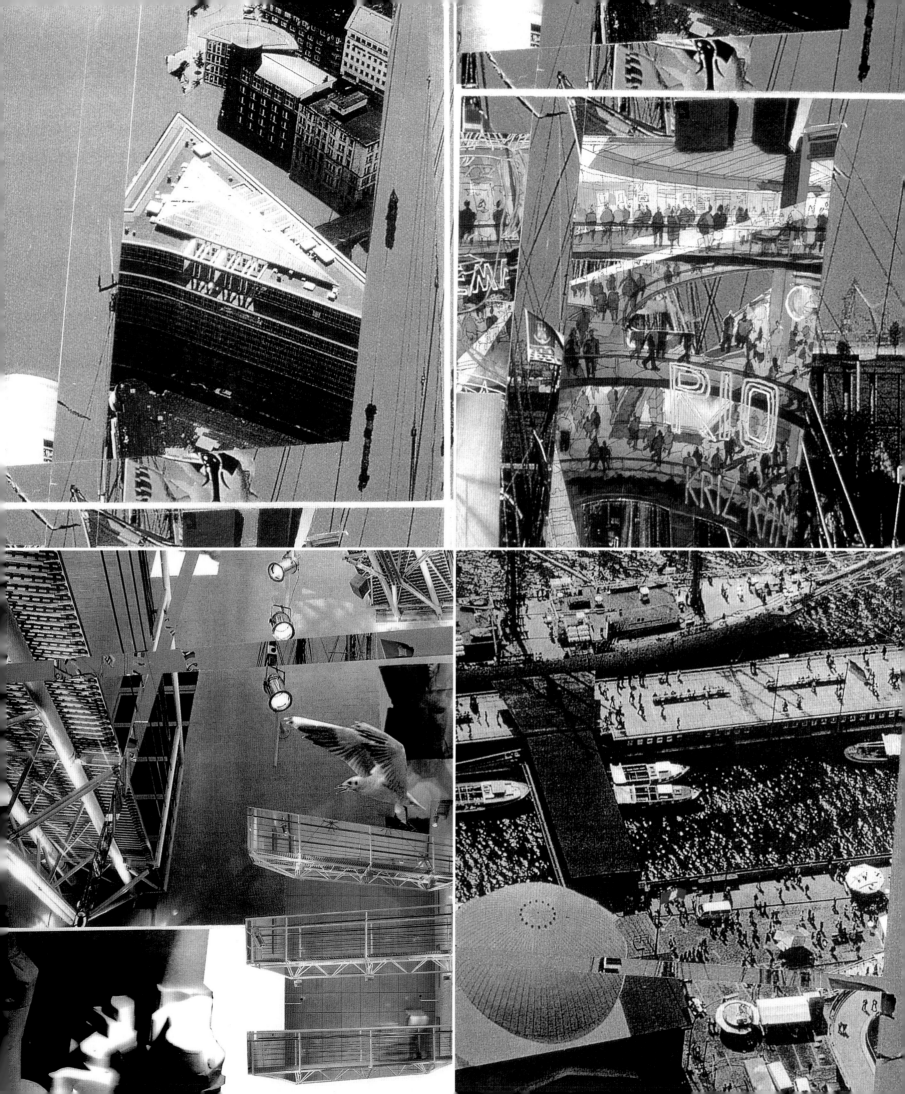

Roppongi 6-6 is a twenty-four-hour, multiuse development with 7 million square feet of office, cultural, residential and retail entertainment buildings, on 28 acres in the midst of an upscale residential area in Tokyo due for completion in 2002. Focusing on the space between buildings to create human-scaled experience and identity, the Jerde Partnership has proposed a stepped circulation path and landscaping as the means to shape a coherent place between free-floating structural elements.

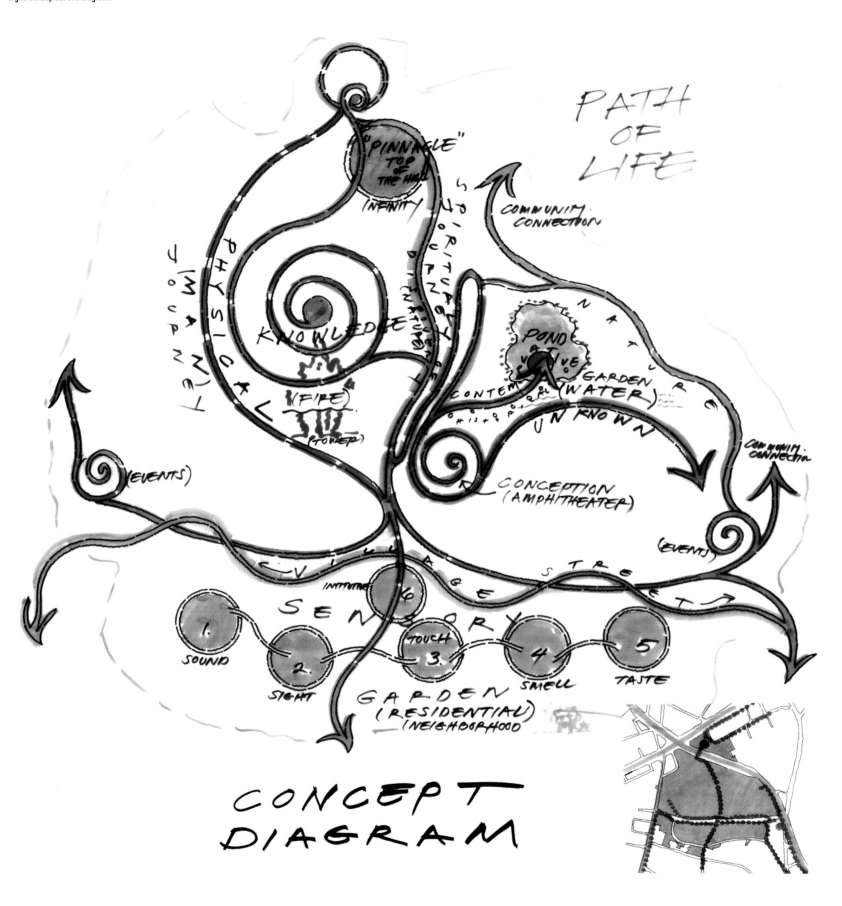

PATH OF LIFE

COMMUNITY CONNECTION

"PINNACLE" TOP OF THE HILL

INFINITY

PHYSICAL JOURNEY

SPIRITUAL JOURNEY

KNOWLEDGE

NATURE JOURNEY

POND & WATERFALL

GARDEN (WATER)

CONTEMPLATION

(FIRE)

(TOWER)

UNKNOWN

COMMUNITY CONNECTION

(EVENTS)

CONCEPTION (AMPHITHEATER)

(EVENTS)

VILLAGE STREETS

SENSORY

INITIATIVE

6

TOUCH

3.

1. SOUND

2. SIGHT

4. SMELL

5. TASTE

GARDEN (RESIDENTIAL) (NEIGHBORHOOD)

CONCEPT DIAGRAM

Left: Plans at eight different levels of the site.

YOU
ARE
HERE
⇩

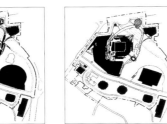 

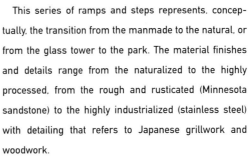

At Roppongi 6-6, the masterplan was developed by the client, the Mori Building Company. The Jerde Partnership has added a non-axial circulation, thereby making connections between the range of functions and singular buildings on the site. The Jerde Partnership is coordinating the Roppongi project team, which includes Kohn Pedersen Fox (KPF), Richard Gluckman Architects, Maki and Associates, CD Partnership, the landscape architects EDAW and Marc Peter Keane. A flexible set of strategies, aimed at keeping the large site coherent without appearing controlled, have been generated by co-creative practices.

At the project's center, a winding corridor, lined with the tiny storefronts of specialist local retailers, descends 50 feet (15 m.) across the site. This pathway begins at the project's arrival plaza, a vast open area that includes a subway station, the Jerde Partnership-designed Hollywood Cosmetics Building and a massive office building designed by KPF, which is the densest tower in Japan. The path descends to the lowest level, where an amphitheater gives way to an Edo-inspired garden.

This series of ramps and steps represents, conceptually, the transition from the manmade to the natural, or from the glass tower to the park. The material finishes and details range from the naturalized to the highly processed, from the rough and rusticated (Minnesota sandstone) to the highly industrialized (stainless steel) with detailing that refers to Japanese grillwork and woodwork.

Circling the KPF-designed tower are two circulation rings of shops and restaurants, and nearby is a European-style avenue destined to become Tokyo's "Rodeo Drive," both also designed by the Jerde Partnership.

Right: Computer rendering of circulation.

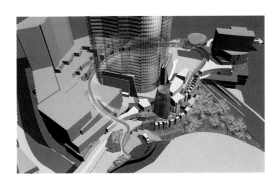

"The spatial is no longer acted upon only by architects, yet architects rarely focus attention on the process that creates——and the conditions that surround——the object or building. Our work also addresses this 'in-between.' Our work synthesizes many disciplines in order to produce the tools needed to advance human community as we move into time." Jon Jerde

Dentsu Headquarters at Shiodome The Shiodome project will be the new Tokyo corporate headquarters for Dentsu—Japan's media and advertising giant. Located in a new district of the city adjacent to Ginza and due for completion in 2002, the project combines an entertainment and commercial base with a 1.8 million square foot tower designed by French architect Jean Nouvel. The base, designed as an all-weather park that encloses a retail entertainment and cultural complex, is seen as a "landscape" that will introduce human-scale to the project and make connections to the surrounding urban area.

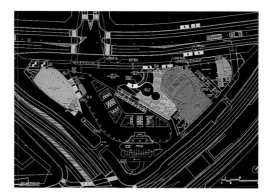

Left: Site plan showing nearby infrastructure.

YOU
ARE
HERE
⇩

Conceptually, the project is seen as a composition of natural rock and smooth crystal. Jean Nouvel's crystalline tower is designed to be an architectural statement that solidifies Dentsu's image. The Jerde Partnership design for the base of the Dentsu Headquarters will be a stepped and curving canyon designed to look as if it has been forged by natural water sources. It is entered via a sunken plaza that serves as a transition between the project's exterior and interior. A curvilinear stair leads from the plaza to a carved-rock crevasse filled with suspended landscaping and cascading waterfalls. This area is an entry portal to entertainment and fashion shops. Dining terraces fold into the sunken garden, concealing a Shiki performing arts theater.

Suspended above the canyon, the glass-enclosed park, has three separate realms: in the upper realm spreading shade trees grow up from the glass roof; the middle realm contains terrarium vine plants; and in the lower realm landscaping grows up from the terrace floors. The two curving glass planes that enclose the park are a transition from Nouvel's glass tower above. Stone walls wrapping the perimeter, expressed in large-scale, cleft-face blocks laid in horizontal ribbons, mimic the natural stratification of the earth's surface.

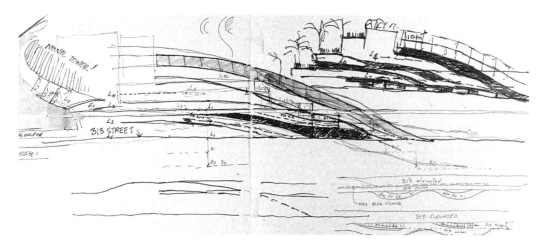

Left: Sketches of the project.

Opposite: Rendered aerial view of Shiodome's base, with glass roof.

Below: Sketch models of glass roof.

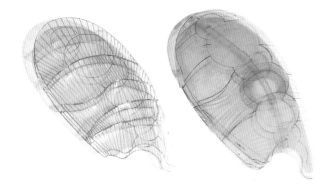

"To a great extent it is the experience of the base that forms our opinions of cities—the bottom forty feet. This is the domain of retail and entertainment." Jon Jerde

Left: Rendered section of base.

Namba is a mixed-use project for the city of Osaka, Japan, with three main elements: a new park, a large-scale canyonlike corridor and a leisure-oriented retail and entertainment complex. The Namba design introduces natural conditions—a large park and a curving canyon—to its urban location in order to provide new connections within the fabric of the city when it is completed in 2003.

YOU
ARE
HERE
⇩

Namba is intended to be a public amenity for an area that has none. The site is an infrastructural hub for the city, adjacent to the Namba train station, which is the first stop on the new line connecting the Kansai Airport to Osaka.

The new verdant, sloping park gradually ascends eight stories from the street. It is a pastoral amenity that contrasts with the hard, bustling environment surrounding it. Groves of trees are interspersed with clusters of rocks, cliffs and outcroppings on a lush lawn. Water features in the park include streams, falls and ponds. A series of large outdoor terraces for dining and exhibition venues afford views of the city.

The most dramatic feature of the project is the linear "canyon" that bifurcates the park plane. Designed as a

corridor connecting the east and west edges of the site, it is the project's main attraction. Filled with trees and outcroppings, coves, caves, valleys and precipices, the canyon criss-crosses the park, intersecting at three points with circular shopping corridors that run through the interiors of the two bifurcated blocks. The intersections of these two circulation spaces—one devoted entirely to amenities, the other to experience—introduces, according to Jon Jerde, moments of "visual and visceral interruption."

Glass-covered bridges will cross from one side of the canyon to the other. By night, they will be arcing tubes of light. All vertical spaces are sky-lit from the park above. At selected locations, varying with each level, direct access from the canyon is provided to the outdoor terraces.

Far left: Site plan of Phase One.

Above left: The internal corridor is modeled on a canyon.

Above right: Model of site.

Opposite: Concept sketches made by Jerde.

Right: Conceptual watercolor by Jon Jerde.

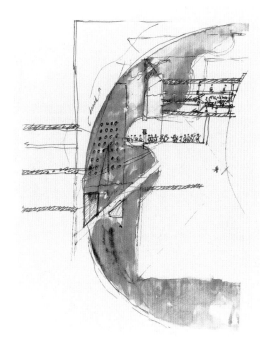

"In separating the shopping center from the housing block, the civic center from the entertainment district, we are left with no common realm, no simultaneity. This has destroyed our kaleidoscopic sense of life and created a tremendous need in the general population to want to come together and experience the restorative energy that is provided by a complex communal experience." Jon Jerde

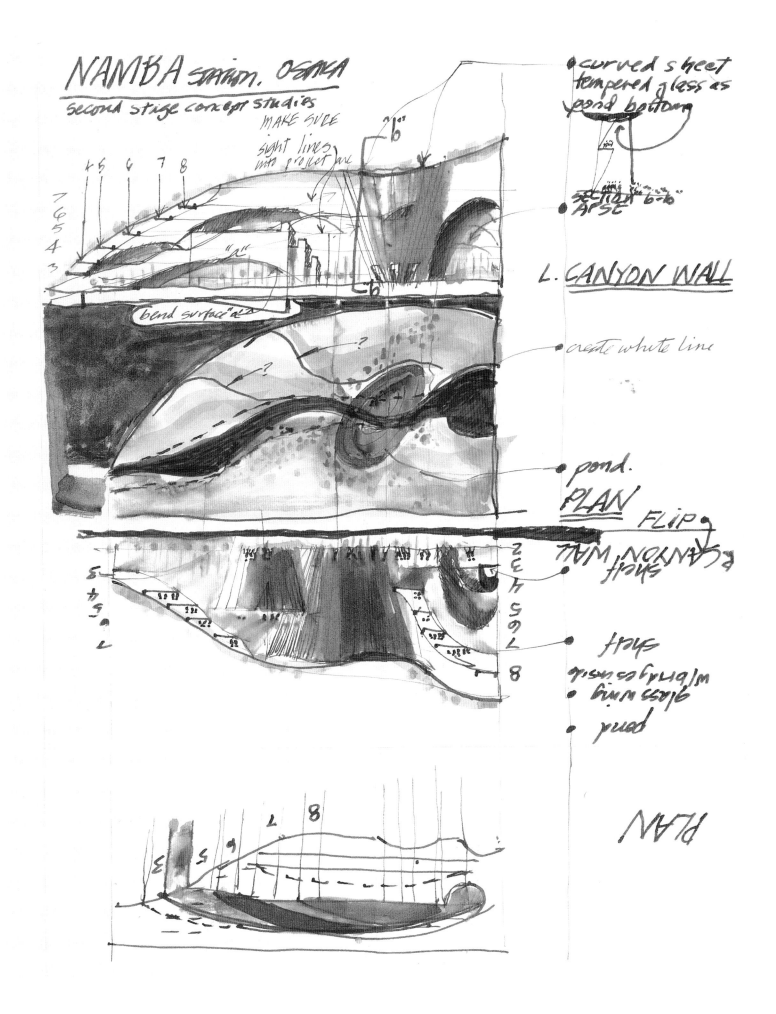

NAMBA STATION, OSAKA

second stage concept studies

MAKE SURE
sight lines
into project arc

• curved sheet
tempered glass as
pond bottom

SECTION b-b
APSE

L. CANYON WALL

• create white line

• pond.

PLAN   FLIP

bend surface "a"

E CANYON WALL
shelf

• shelf

• glass wing
w/bright glass trim

• pond

PLAN

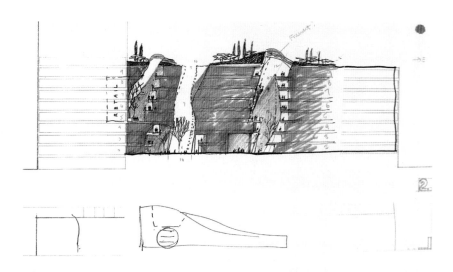

This page: Watercolor sketch
sections and plan by Jon Jerde.

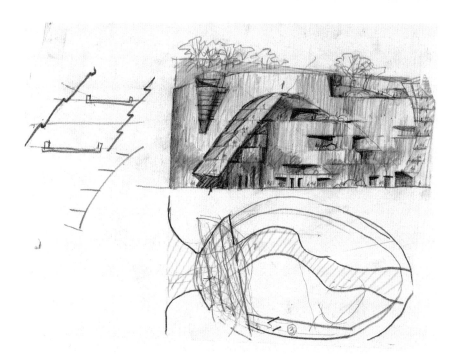

This page: Conceptual plan diagrams showing internal circulation patterns.

This page and opposite:
Rendered watercolors of
circulation canyon.

NAMBA CANYON STUDY

Zlota Centre Sited near the monumental Palace of Culture and the Warszawa Centralna train station, Zlota Centre is a mixed-use retail and entertainment center intended to restore Warsaw's urban identity. Using landscape as its primary organizer, inspired by the city's historic parks and public squares, the project, intended to act as a spatial and cultural connector, reuniting the ruptured fabric of the city, will be completed in 2003.

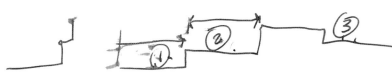

YOU ARE HERE ⇩

At Zlota Centre, free-market consumerism, in the form of a retail entertainment center and public park commissioned by a Dutch real-estate company, confronts the remains of the Communist state. The project is being built in the shadow of the Palace of Culture and Science, which was designed by Russian architect Lev Rudniev and erected in the early 1950s as a gift from the Soviet Union to the people of Warsaw.

The challenge for the Jerde Partnership is to make a connection between the disproportionately monumental Palace and the historical pedestrian-scale urban topography, still extant despite the damage caused by World War II. The firm's main urban design strategy makes connections in design, scale and plan to the surrounding environment, yet the project retains its own character within.

Zlota Centre's urban armature is on axis with the Palace of Culture, and the exterior mirrors the monumentality of the Soviet era building. The interior, which Jerde describes as "a sinuous multileveled canyon of retail," is a lively place, which connects to an enclosed, landscaped 7.4-acre (3 ha.) park. The park, protected from the weather by a glass roof, consists of recreational zones. The program for the 330,000 square foot (31,000 s.m.) mixed-use Zlota Centre consists of hotels, office, residential, entertainment, food and retail. The office, housing and hotel functions are located in mid- and high-rise towers encircling the public center.

Above: Sketch diagram of site section showing connection to existing city center.

Opposite, above: Diagrammatic plans of levels one and two.

Opposite, below: Longitudinal section with Palace of Culture in the background.

Left: Site plan showing Palace of Culture.

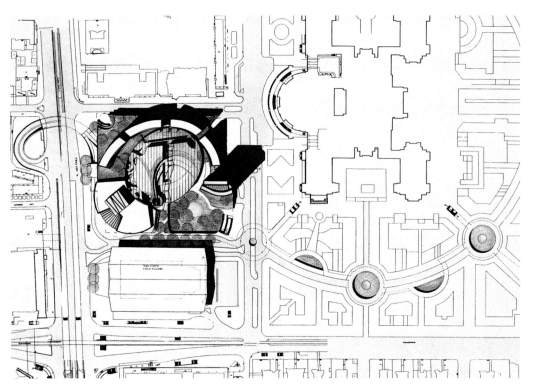

"Our projects are always the beginning of something." Jon Jerde

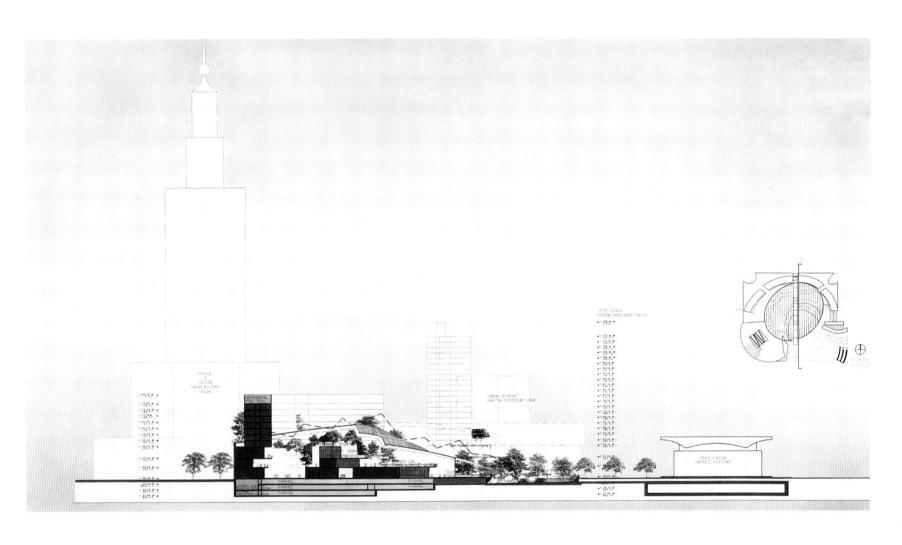

Los Angeles Olympic Games
Los Angeles, California, USA
DATE
Start date 1982
Finish date 1984
PROJECT TYPE
Urban planning and architecture
SITE AREA
100-mile radius of downtown Los Angeles
COMPONENTS
75 Olympic sports and Arts Festival venues
10 freeway systems (environmental graphics)
30 boulevards (environmental graphics)
12 transportation centers
3 Olympic villages
CLIENT
The Los Angeles Olympic Organizing
    Committee, Los Angeles, California, USA
PROJECT TEAM
MASTERPLANNING AND ENVIRONMENTAL
    DESIGN
The Jerde Partnership International, Inc.
GRAPHIC DESIGN
Sussman/Prejza
ARCHITECTS, DESIGNERS, ARTISTS AND
    CONSULTANTS
John Aleksich & Associates
Brian and Susan Anuskewics
Archisystem
Beck & Graboski Design Office
Daniel Benjamin
Pamela Burton & Company
Vitto Cetta & Associates
Communication Arts + Michael Jurdan Inc.
Daniel, Mann, Johnson & Mendenhall
Annette del Zoppo Productions
The Design Works
EDAW, Inc.
The Feola/Deenihan Partnership, Inc.
Glenwood L. Garvey & Associates
Doron Gazit
Hinsche & Associates
Gere Kavanaugh Designs
LAX Studios
TW Layman Associates
Albert C. Martin & Associates
Neuhart/Donges/Neuhart Designers Inc.
Peridian Group
Barton Phelps & Associates
POD
Rachlin/Roberts Architects AIA, Inc.
Michael Sanchez Design Associates
Victor Schumacher Architect
Peter Shire
Judi Skalsky, Communications and Media
Skidmore, Owings & Merrill
Greg Spiess, AIA
Jan Steward
Lois Swirnoff
Randall Walker

Ware & Malcolm Architects, Inc.
Emmet L. Wemple & Associates
Ted Wu Design Consultants
COST
US$10 million
AWARDS
Honor Award, AIA, 1985
Special Award for Excellence in the Allied Arts,
    American Institute of Architects (AIA),
    California Council, 1984
Special Citation, American Institute of Graphic
    Arts, 1985
Certificate of Commendation, Board of
    Supervisors, County of Los Angeles, 1984
Special Award, Los Angeles Beautiful, 1984

Horton Plaza
San Diego, California, USA
DATE
Start date 1977
Finish date 1985
PROJECT TYPE
Mixed-use retail and entertainment
SITE AREA
11.5 acres/4.6 hectares
COMPONENTS
Total building area 1.5 million s.f./139,400 m²
Retail (140 shops) 890,000 s.f./82,700 m²
Food court 13,436 s.f./1,250 m²
Restaurants 20,685 s.f./1,900 m²
Office 250,000 s.f./23,225 m²
Cinemas (14) 8,500 s.f./790 m²
Hotel (452 rooms) 576,334 s.f./53,540 m²
Stage theaters 40,300 s.f./3,740 m²
Residential 66 apartments
Parking 2,170 spaces
CLIENT
The Hahn Company, San Diego, California, USA
PROJECT TEAM
DESIGN ARCHITECT
The Jerde Partnership International, Inc.
ASSOCIATE ARCHITECT/NORDSTROM
The Callison Partnership
GRAPHIC DESIGNERS
Sussman/Prejza
STRUCTURAL ENGINEER
Robert Englekirk Inc.
ELECTRICAL ENGINEER
Store, Matakovich & Wolfberg
MECHANICAL ENGINEER
David Chen & Associates
CIVIL ENGINEERS
Paller Roberts Engineering
LANDSCAPE ARCHITECT
Wimmer Yamada & Associates
SOILS ENGINEER
Leighton & Associates
ART CONSULTANT
Fine Arts Services, Inc.
PARKING CONSULTANT
Sy-Art Concrete Construction
FIRE AND SAFETY CODES

Rolf Jensen & Associates
PLANNING CONSULTANT
Gustafson Poulsen & Associates
SPECIFICATIONS CONSULTANT
Darby Sanchis Associates
GENERAL CONTRACTOR
NuHahn, Inc.
COST
US$140 million (construction)
US$204 million (Incl. department stores)
ATTENDANCE FIGURES
1985: 25 million
(average annual: 18 million)
AWARDS
Merit Award, AIA, Los Angeles chapter, 1986
Citation, AIA, San Diego chapter, 1982

New Port City
Jersey City, New Jersey, USA
DATE
Start date 1986
Finish date 1986
PROJECT TYPE
Masterplan for an urban district
SITE AREA
400 acres/162 hectares
COMPONENTS
Total building area 90 million s.f./8.4 million m²
Harbors
Waterfronts
Waterfront boulevards
Yacht clubs
Trade marts
Low- and high-rise residential
Offices
Retail
Hotel
Cultural, including museums
CLIENT
Melvin Simon & Associates, Sam LeFrak
PROJECT TEAM
DESIGN ARCHITECT
The Jerde Partnership International, Inc.
STATUS
Conceptual design

Satellite New Town
Near Paris, France
DATE
Start date 1985
Finish date 1986
PROJECT TYPE
Masterplan for a new city
SITE AREA
1.5 million s.f./139,400 m²
COMPONENTS
Culture and amusement zones
Entertainment
Retail
International design center
Hotels
Spas

Conference center
CLIENT
Confidential
PROJECT TEAM
DESIGN ARCHITECT
The Jerde Partnership International, Inc.
STATUS
Conceptual design

Rinku Masterplan and Town
Block III
Osaka, Japan
DATE
Start date 1988
Finish date 1989
PROJECT TYPE
Masterplan for an urban district
SITE AREA
Masterplan 700 acres/283 hectares
Block III 10.7 acres/4.3 hectares
COMPONENTS
Retail/entertainment facilities 1.3 million
    s.f./120,000 m²
Cultural facilities 320,000 s.f./30,000 m²
World business center/office tower 1.2 million
    s.f./115,000 m²
Hotel
Canal 44,000 s.f./4,000 m²
Parking spaces 2,220
CLIENT
Nippon Life Insurance Company (Nissay)
PROJECT TEAM
DESIGN ARCHITECT
The Jerde Partnership International, Inc.
ASSOCIATE ARCHITECT
Nikken Sekkei
STATUS
Schematic design

Del Mar Plaza
Del Mar, Southern California,
USA
DATE
Start date 1985
Finish date 1989
PROJECT TYPE
Mixed-use (specialty retail)
SITE AREA
2.5 acres/1 hectare
COMPONENTS
Total building area 250,000 s.f./23,200 m²
Gross leasable area 75,000 s.f./6,900 m²
Retail 46,400 s.f./4,300 m²
Marketplace 9,000 s.f./830 m²
Restaurants 14,400 s.f./1,300 m²
Public spaces 160,000 s.f./14,800 m²
Parking spaces 350
CLIENT
Del Mar Partnership, Inc., Del Mar, California
PROJECT TEAM
DESIGN ARCHITECT
The Jerde Partnership International, Inc.

EXECUTIVE ARCHITECT
McCabe/Gish Architects
STRUCTURAL ENGINEER
Safino, Butcher, Ormonde
MECHANICAL AND ELECTRICAL ENGINEER
Ila + Zammit Engineering Group
LANDSCAPE ARCHITECT
Emmet L. Wemple & Associates
GENERAL CONTRACTOR
Ninteman Construction Inc.
COST
US$28 million (construction)
US$33 million
AWARDS
Award for Excellence, Urban Land Institute,
    1991

Luminaire
Houston, Texas, USA
DATE
Start date 1988
Finish date 1989
PROJECT TYPE
Masterplan for an urban entertainment-
    retail center
COMPONENTS
Total building area 450,000 s.f./41,000 m²
Retail
Theaters
Imax theater
Nightclubs
Entertainment
CLIENT
Skywalker Corporation
PROJECT TEAM
DESIGN ARCHITECT
The Jerde Partnership International, Inc.
STATUS
Conceptual design

Fashion Island
Newport Beach, California, USA
DATE
Start date 1987
Finish date 1989
PROJECT TYPE
Renovation of regional shopping center
SITE AREA
87 acres/35 hectares
COMPONENTS
Total building area (gross building area) 1.3
    million s.f./125,400 m²
Gross leasable area 1.2 million s.f./111,500 m²
Parking 5,800 spaces
CLIENT
Irvine Retail Properties, Newport Beach,
    California
PROJECT TEAM
DESIGN ARCHITECT
The Jerde Partnership International, Inc.
ASSOCIATE ARCHITECT, ATRIUM COURT
Kober Associates

ASSOCIATE ARCHITECT, STORES
Ellerbe Becket
ASSOCIATE ARCHITECT, PLAZAS
Sasaki-Walker
STRUCTURAL ENGINEER
Robert Englekirk Incorporated
MECHANICAL ENGINEER
David Chen & Associates
ELECTRICAL ENGINEER
Store, Matakovich & Wolfberg
LANDSCAPE ARCHITECT
The SWA Group
GENERAL CONTRACTOR, PHASE I AND II
HCB Contractors
GENERAL CONTRACTOR, PHASE III
Robert E. Bayley Construction
COST
US$100 million

Urbanopolis
Anaheim, California, USA
DATE
Start date 1990
Finish date 1996
PROJECT TYPE
Masterplan
COMPONENTS
Total building area 4.3 million s.f./404,000 m²
Theme hotels (2,000 rooms) 1.3 million
    s.f./120,800 m²
Retail shops 400,000s.f./37,000 m²
Eating and drinking 145,000 s.f./13,400 m²
Theaters 80,000 s.f./7,400 m²
Attractions 40,000 s.f./3,700 m²
Residential 1.1 million s.f./102,200 m²
Garden offices 1.2 million s.f./111,500 m²
Conference center 45,000 s.f./4,100 m²
Sports and health club 40,000 s.f./3,700 m²
CLIENT
Wrather Corporation and The Disney
    Development Company
PROJECT TEAM
DESIGN ARCHITECT
The Jerde Partnership International, Inc.
STATUS
Conceptual design

Makuhari Town Center
Chiba, Japan
DATE
Start date 1993
Finish date 1993
PROJECT TYPE
Masterplan for a town center
SITE AREA
5 acres/2 hectares
COMPONENTS
Retail
Entertainment
Community Center
Health facilities
Television Studio

CLIENT
Mitsubishi Real Estate
PROJECT TEAM
DESIGN ARCHITECT
The Jerde Partnership International, Inc.
PROJECT ARCHITECT
Mitsubishi Jisho
STATUS
Conceptual design

Mall of America
Bloomington, Minnesota, USA
DATE
Start date 1989
Finish date 1992
PROJECT TYPE
Retail and family entertainment complex
SITE AREA
78 acres/31 hectares
COMPONENTS
GBA 4.2 million s.f./390,300 m²
GLA 2.5 million s.f./232,300 m²
Department stores (4) 900,000 s.f./83,600 m²
Mall stores (350) 1.6 million s.f./148,600 m²
Restaurants 30
Cinemas 14
Nightclubs/entertainment 90,000 s.f./8,300 m²
Lego imagination center 5,000 s.f./460 m²
Two-level miniature golf mountain
Knott's Camp Snoopy 7 acres/2.8 hectares
Parking spaces 12,750
CLIENT
Mall of America Co., a subsidiary of Melvin
    Simon & Associates, Inc., Indianapolis, and
    Triple Five Corp Ltd, Edmonton, Alberta
PROJECT TEAM
DESIGN ARCHITECT, MALL OF AMERICA
The Jerde Partnership International, Inc.
DESIGN ARCHITECT, KNOTT'S CAMP SNOOPY
Robin Hall, Knott's Berry Farm, Buena Park
PROJECT ARCHITECT, MALL OF AMERICA
HGA/KKE, an association of Hammel Green
    Abrahamson Inc., and Korunsky Kran
    Erickson Architects, Inc.
PROJECT ARCHITECT, LEGO
Jeter, Cook & Jepson
COMPETITION DESIGN ARCHITECT
Maurice Sunderland Architecture, Inc.
COST US$625 million
ATTENDANCE FIGURES
Average 40 million visitors per year

Rokko Island
Kobe, Japan
DATE
Start date 1991
Finish date 1992
PROJECT TYPE
Masterplan for a marine city
SITE AREA
10.4 million s.f./970,000 m²
COMPONENTS

Market place 980,000 s.f./92,000 m²
Life Design Complex 10 million s.f./100,000 m²
Culture, community 86,000 s.f./8,000 m²
Convention hotel 1,290,000 s.f./120,000 m²
Office 480,000s.f./45,000 m²
Research complex 590,000 s.f./55,000 m²
Specialty school/college 215,000 s.f./20,000 m²
Housing 5.16 million s.f./480,000 m²
Parking spaces 9,000
CLIENT
Daiwa House Industry Co, Ltd
Chuo Trust Bank
NTT Data Communications Systems Corp
Takashimaya Department Store
Toppan Printing Co, Ltd
Ebara Corporation
PROJECT TEAM
DESIGN ARCHITECT, PLANNING
The Jerde Partnership International, Inc.
PRODUCTION COORDINATION
Tech R & DS Co., LTD
CONCEPT
Nippon Arts, Inc.
PROGRAMMING
A & A Planners Associates Co.
ARCHITECTURAL CONSULTANT
Zeal Xebec Co., LTD
INTERNATIONAL LIAISON
PAL International
STATUS
Conceptual design

Universal City Masterplan &
Universal CityWalk
Universal City, California, USA
DATE
Masterplan start date 1989
CityWalk start date 1991
Phase One finish date 1993
Phase Two finish date 2000
PROJECT TYPE
Masterplan for a mixed-use entertainment
    district
SITE AREA
Masterplan 425 acres/172 hectares
Phase One 20 acres/8 hectares
Phase Two 3.25 acres/1.3 hectares
COMPONENTS
Masterplan
Office 8.6 million s.f./801,634 m²
Retail/entertainment 1.2 million s.f./114,917 m²
Cultural 120,000 s.f./11,148 m²
Hospitality 875,000 s.f./81,287 m²
Parking 37,455 spaces
Phase One
Total building area 451,585 s.f./41,900 m²
Retail 55,220 s.f./5,100 m²
Restaurants 87,434 s.f./8,125 m²
Entertainment/film 130,000 s.f./12,000 m²
Offices/classrooms 178,931 s.f./15,600 m²
Parking spaces 5,200
Phase Two

Total building area 87,250 s.f./8,100 m²
Retail 36,000 s.f./3,340 m²
Restaurants 26,250 s.f./2,440 m²
Entertainment/film 25,000 s.f./2,320 m²
CLIENT
Masterplan MCA Development Co.
Phase One MCA Development Co.
Phase Two Universal Creative, Universal
    Studios, Universal City, California USA
PROJECT TEAM, MASTERPLAN
MASTERPLANNER
The Jerde Partnership International, Inc.
INFRASTRUCTURE MASTERPLANNER
DMJM/Keating
MATERIALS HANDLING MANAGER
Cini-Little International, Inc.
LANDSCAPE ARCHITECT
Emmet L. Wemple & Associates
HARDWARE CONSULTANT
Finish Hardware Specifiers
BILLBOARD CONSULTANT
Gannett Outdoor
SIGNAGE AND GRAPHICS CONSULTANT
Harmonica
SPECIALTY LIGHTING CONSULTANT
Imero Fiorentino Associates
PARKING CONSULTANT
International Parking Design
CIVIL ENGINEER
IWA Engineers
ELEVATOR CONSULTANT
John Hess & Associates
TRAFFIC ENGINEERING CONSULTANT
Linscott, Law and Greenspan
ROOFING CONSULTANT
Manville Roof Construction Management
ENVIRONMENTAL ASSESSMENTS
    CONSULTANT
Myra Frank & Associates
SPACE-FRAME CONSULTANT
Pearce Structures
FIRE PROTECTION CONSULTANT
Rolf Jensen & Associates
MICROCLIMATE CONSULTANT
Rowan Williams Davies & Irwin Inc.
SIGNAGE AND GRAPHICS CONSULTANT
Wayne Hunt Design, Inc.
CITYWALK, PHASE ONE AND PHASE TWO
DESIGN ARCHITECT
The Jerde Partnership International, Inc.
EXECUTIVE ARCHITECT
DMJM/Keating
ASSOCIATE ARCHITECT, CENTRAL COURT
SITE
ASSOCIATE ARCHITECT, PANASONIC
Hodgetts + Fung Design Associates
ASSOCIATE ARCHITECT, MTV
Morphosis
ASSOCIATE ARCHITECT, EASTWALK
Anderson and Schwartz
ASSOCIATE ARCHITECT, SHOWSCAN THEATER
Ellerbe Becket

ASSOCIATE ARCHITECT, IMAX
Hardy Holzman Pfeiffer Associates
LANDSCAPE ARCHITECT
Emmet L. Wemple & Associates
LIGHTING DESIGNER
Imero Fiorentino Associates
WATER ELEMENTS DESIGNER
WET Design
CIVIL ENGINEER
IWA Engineers
TRAFFIC ENGINEER
Linscott, Law & Greenspan, Engineers
GRAPHIC DESIGNER
OLIO
GENERAL CONTRACTOR
Ray Wilson Company
COST
Phase One US$55 million
Phase Two US$22 million
AWARDS
Award of Excellence, The Asian American
    Architects and Engineers Association, 1997
Design Award, International Council of
    Shopping Centers, 1994
Urban Beautification Award, Los Angeles
    Business Council, 1994

The Fremont Street Experience
Las Vegas, Nevada, USA
DATE
Start date 1992
Finish date 1995
PROJECT TYPE
Urban design entertainment district
SITE AREA
5 acres/2 hectares
COMPONENTS
"SPACE FRAME"
Length 1,400 ft./ 426 m.
Width 100 ft./30.4 m.
Height 100 ft./30.4 m.
"SKY PARADE"
Lights 2.1 million
Computers 32
Sound 540,000-watt system, 40 speakers
Parking 1,400 new spaces
Retail 40,000 s.f./3,700 m²
Office 8,000 s.f./743 m²
CLIENT
The Fremont Street Experience Limited
    Liability Co.
PROJECT TEAM
DESIGN ARCHITECT
The Jerde Partnership International, Inc.
ASSOCIATE ARCHITECT
Harry Campbell Architects
ARCHITECT, PARKING STRUCTURE
Mary Kozlowski Architect Inc.
CONSTRUCTION MANAGER
Marnell Corrao Associates
SHOW DESIGNER
Jeremy Railton & Associates

COST
US$70 million
ATTENDANCE FIGURES
Average 18 million visitors per annum
AWARDS
Merit Award, Urban Design, AIA, Los Angeles
    chapter, 1996
Outstanding Design Award, Themed
    Entertainment Association (THEA), 1996

Santa Fe Town Center
Mexico City, Mexico
DATE
Start date 1994
Finish date 1995
PROJECT TYPE
Masterplan and concept design for
    new community
SITE AREA
2,100 acres/850 hectares
COMPONENTS
Total building area 2.9 million s.f./270,000 m²
Project site area 968,760 s.f./90,000 m²
Office 1,668,420 s.f./155,000 m²
Residential 1,180,000 s.f./110,000 m²
Retail/commercial 247,572 s.f./23,000 m²
Cinema 75,348 s.f./7,000 m²
Hotel 355,212 s.f./33,000 m²
CLIENT
Reichmann International
ICA-Reichmann Santa Fe SA de CV
ICA
PROJECT TEAM
MASTERPLANNER, DESIGN ARCHITECT
The Jerde Partnership International, Inc. with
    artist Robert Graham
EXECUTIVE ARCHITECT
Haldeman Powell + Partners
Haldeman Powell de Mexico, SA de CV
ASSOCIATE ARCHITECT
August H Alvarez Arquitecto Y Asociados SC
STRUCTURAL ENGINEER
Brockette Davis Drake, Inc.
HVAC ENGINEER
DYPRO
PLUMBING ENGINEER
Garza & Maldonada
ELECTRICAL ENGINEER
ICI
MEP LOCAL CONSULTANT
TMP/MBI
HVAC CONSULTANT
The Mitchell Partnership
ELECTRICAL CONSULTANT/COMMUNICATION
Mulvey & Banani International
TRAFFIC CONSULTANT
Carter & Burgess
CIVIL ENGINEER
Robert Bein, William Frost & Associates
PARKING CONSULTANT
BA Group
RESIDENTIAL ARCHITECT

Kaplan/McLaughlin/Diaz
LANDSCAPE ARCHITECT
Hanna Olin
STRUCTURAL CONSULTANT
Alonso Garcia & Asociados, SC
GEO-TECH CONSULTANT
TGC Geotechnia
ICA-SOLUM
ENVIRONMENTAL CONSULTANT
Dames & Moore
ELEVATOR CONSULTANT
Katz Drago & Co.
WIND CONSULTANT
Boundary Layer Wind Tunnel Laboratory
STATUS
Schematic design

Robina Town Centre
Queensland, Australia
DATE
Start date 1991
Finish date 1996
PROJECT TYPE
Masterplan and mixed-use town center
SITE AREA
86 acres/35 hectares
COMPONENTS
Total building area 1.34 million s.f./124,650 m²
Retail 1 million s.f./93,000 m²
Entertainment 7,500 s.f./700 m²
Restaurants 80,700 s.f./7,500 m²
Office 49,000 s.f./4,550 m²
Cinemas 32,200 s.f./3,000 m²
Commercial 103,000 s.f./9,600 m²
Parking spaces 6,000
CLIENT
Robina Land Corporation Pty, Ltd
PROJECT TEAM
DESIGN ARCHITECT
The Jerde Partnership International, Inc.
EXECUTIVE ARCHITECT
Cameron Chisholm & Nicol
WATER FEATURES DESIGNER
WET Design
LANDSCAPE ARCHITECT
EDAW, Inc.
LIGHTING
Barry Webb & Associates
GRAPHIC DESIGNER
Dot Dash
COST
US$141 million
AWARDS
Commendation, Royal Australian Institute of
    Architects, Queensland chapter, 1998

Beursplein
Rotterdam, The Netherlands
DATE
Start date 1992
Finish date 1996
PROJECT TYPE

Multi-use urban development
SITE AREA
3/4 acres/1.35 hectares
COMPONENTS
Retail 328,302 s.f./57,000 m²
Residential tower 143,161 s.f./13,300 m²
Parking garage 109,793 s.f./13,000 m²
Technical 10,760 s.f./1,000 m²
metro station access
CLIENT
Multi Vastgoed b.v.
PROJECT TEAM
PROJECT ARCHITECTS
The Jerde Partnership International, Inc.
PROJECT ARCHITECTS
T+T Design
De Architekten cie
Architectenbureau D&T van Manen
Van Moort & Partners Architectenbureau
KRAAIJVANGER Urbis Bureau voor
    Architectuur
PRINCIPALS
Consortium Beursplein (Municipality of
    Rotterdam/ING VASTGOED/Focas b.v.)
C&A
Kreymborg
Hema
Vroom & Dreesmann
LIGHTING CONSULTANT
Gallegos Lighting
ENVIRONMENTAL GRAPHICS DESIGNER
Environmental Image
COST
US$145 million
AWARDS
Design Award, Innovative Design and
    Construction of a new project, International
Council of Shopping Centers, 1998
The Netherlands Honor Award, 1997
Merit Award, Urban Design, Los Angeles
    chapter, 1997
Shopping Center Award, European
    International Council of Shopping Centres,
    1997
Bouwbeurs 1997 (Dutch construction prize),
    International Building and Construction
    Exhibition

Canal City Hakata
Fukuoka, Japan
DATE
Start date 1987
Finish date 1996
PROJECT TYPE
Urban mixed-use development
SITE AREA
373,800 s.f./34,748 m²
COMPONENTS
Total building area 2,583,360 s.f./240,000 m²
Luxury hotel (400 rms) 505,908 s.f./47,000 m²
Business hotel 129,168 s.f./12,000 m²
Retail 473,616 s.f./44,000 m²

Commercial showrooms 75,348 s.f./7,000 m²
Office 441,324 s.f./41,000 m²
Performing arts theater 91,494 s.f./8,500 m²
Cineplex 113,022 s.f.,10,500 m²
Entertainment 102,258 s.f./9,500 m²
Restaurants 80,730 s.f./7,500 m²
Parking spaces 1,550
CLIENT
Sumitomo Life Insurance Company
Fukuoka Jisho Co., Ltd.
Fukuoka Japan, Urban Design and
    Development Co.
PROJECT TEAM
DESIGN ARCHITECT
The Jerde Partnership International, Inc.
ASSOCIATE ARCHITECT
Fukuoka Jisho Co., Ltd., Urban Design and
    Development Co.
GENERAL CONTRACTORS
The Zenitaka Corporation
Shimizu Corporation
Obayashi Corporation
Fujita Corporation
LANDSCAPE ARCHITECT
EDAW, Inc.
ENVIRONMENTAL, MERCHANDISE DESIGNER
Clifford Selbert Design Collaborative
WATER FEATURES DESIGNER
WET Design
LIGHTING DESIGNER
Joe Kaplan Architectural Lighting
ART CONSULTANT
Fine Arts Services, Inc.
COST
US$1.4 billion
ATTENDANCE FIGURES
1996–7 (first year): 16.4 million
AWARDS
Merit Award, Urban Design, AIA, California
    Council, 1998
Merit Award, Urban Design, Los Angeles
    chapter, 1997
International Design and Development Award,
    International Council of Shopping Centers,
    1997
Fukuoka Urban Beautification Award, Mayor,
    City of Fukuoka, 1997
Gold Nugget Grand Award, Pacific Coast
    Builders Conference/Western Building
    Show, 1997
Grand Award: Best Commercial Project—
    Retail, Pacific Coast Builders Conference,
    1997
The Display Design Award, Japanese Society
    of Commercial Space Designers, 1996
Gold Prize for Good Design, Japanese Ministry
    of International Trade and Industry, 1996
Urban Landscape Award, Japanese Ministry of
    Construction and Urban Public Design
    Center, 1996
Best New Facility Award, named by Nikkei
    Shimbun one of two top news events, 1996

Bellagio
Las Vegas, Nevada, USA
DATE
Start date 1994
Finish date 1998
PROJECT TYPE
Resort hotel
SITE AREA
126 acres/51 hectares
COMPONENTS
Total building area 4 million s.f./370,000 m²
35-story hotel tower (3,000 guest rooms), nine
    villas 2 million s.f./185,800 m²
Waterfront village and terraces
    (restaurant and retail district)
Porte-cochere
Retail promenade
Conservatory
Registration courtyard
Exteriors for public space and streets
    (pool area, people mover, vehicular
    entrances)
Nine-acre man-made lake
CLIENT
Mirage Resorts, Inc.
PROJECT TEAM
DESIGN ARCHITECT
The Jerde Partnership International, Inc.
PLANNING ARCHITECT
Atlandia Design
EXECUTIVE ARCHITECT
Anthony A. Marnell II, Chtd.
INTERIOR DESIGNER
Thomas Design Group
ENVIRONMENTAL DESIGNER
OLIO
LANDSCAPE ARCHITECT
Lifescapes International
WATER FEATURES DESIGNER
WET Design
LIGHTING DESIGNER, INTERIOR AND RETAIL
    PROMENADE
Joe Kaplan Architectural Lighting
LIGHTING DESIGNER, EXTERIOR
DHA Lighting
COST
US$1.9 billion

The Gateway
Salt Lake City, Utah, USA
DATE
Start date 1998
Finish date 2002
PROJECT TYPE
Urban, mixed-use redevelopment district
SITE AREA
26 acres/105 hectares
COMPONENTS
Entertainment, retail 675,000 s.f./62,700 m²
Cultural 100,000 s.f./9,200 m²
Office 400,000 s.f./37,000 m²
Residential (700 units) 770,000 s.f./71,000 m²

Hotel (300 rooms) 275,000 s.f./25,000 m²
Parking spaces 4,000
CLIENT
The Boyer Company
PROJECT TEAM
DESIGN ARCHITECT
The Jerde Partnership International, Inc.
RESIDENTIAL ARCHITECT
DiMella Shaffer Associates, Inc.
HOTEL ARCHITECT
Flatow Moore Shaffer McCabe
LANDSCAPE ARCHITECT
EDAW, Inc.
BLOCK A ARCHITECT
Gilles Stransky Brems Smith
CONSULTING ARCHITECTS
MHTN Architects, Inc.
Humphreys & Partners Architects
GRAPHIC DESIGNER
Sussman/Prejza
Elixir Design Incorporated
LIGHTING DESIGNER
Joe Kaplan Architectural Lighting
WATER FEATURES DESIGNER
WET Design
STRUCTURAL ENGINEER
Dunn Associates, Inc.
MECHANICAL ENGINEER
Colvin Engineering
ELECTRICAL ENGINEER
JSH & Associates
CIVIL ENGINEER
Van Boerum & Frank Associates
SOILS ENGINEER
Dames & Moore
COST
US$210 million
STATUS
Design development

One Reeperbahn
Hamburg, Germany
DATE
Start date 1997
Finish date 2001
PROJECT TYPE
Mixed-use entertainment center
SITE AREA
58,000 s.f./5,400 m²
COMPONENTS
Total building area 322,000 s.f./30,000 m²
Cinema 64,500 s.f./6,000 m²
Hotel 64,500 s.f./6,000 m²
IMAX cinema 24,700 s.f./2,300 m²
Entertainment-oriented retail 193,600 s.f./
    18,000 m²
Restaurants
CLIENT
Jackson Commercial BV
PROJECT TEAM
DESIGN ARCHITECT
The Jerde Partnership International, Inc.

STATUS

Design development

Roppongi 6-6
Tokyo, Japan

DATE

Start date 1994

Finish date 2002

PROJECT TYPE

Mixed-use urban district

SITE AREA

28.4 acres/11.5 hectares

COMPONENTS

Total GBA: 6,536,977 s.f./607,300 m²

GLA 958,425 s.f./89,073 m²

Retail 489,580 s.f./45,500 m²

Food 140,030 s.f./13,014 m²

Hotels 560,445 s.f./52,086 m²

Entertainment 66,281 s.f./6,160 m²

Culture 162,207 s.f./15,075 m²

Office 3,017,028 s.f./280,393 m²

Hollywood Building

   Retail 53,358 s.f./4,595 m²

   Entertainment

   Other121,900 s.f./11,329 m²

Asahi TV 4,723 s.f./439 m²

   Retail 4,723 s.f./439 m²

   Culture 670,552 s.f./62,319 m²

   Other 670,552 s.f./62,319 m²

Residential 131,960 s.f./12,264 m²

Other 176,248 s.f./16,380 m²

CLIENT

Mori Building Co., Ltd

PROJECT TEAM

MASTERPLANNER, RETAIL DESIGNER

The Jerde Partnership International, Inc. with

   Mori Building Co.

ARCHITECT OF SUBWAY STATION; ENTRY

   PLAZA; HOLLYWOOD COSMETICS BUILDING;

   WEST LOOP; EAST LOOP; EAST-WEST

   STREET; BLOCK C OFFICE BUILDING;

   BLOCK C RETAIL PODIUM; PARK

The Jerde Partnership International, Inc.

DESIGN ARCHITECT, TOWER BUILDING, HOTEL

Kohn Pedersen Fox Associates PC

Mori Museum

PROJECT ARCHITECT, HOTEL

Mori Building Company

DESIGN ARCHITECT, MORI MUSEUM

Richard Gluckman Architects

DESIGN ARCHITECT, ASAHI TV BUILDING

Maki and Associates

PROJECT ARCHITECT, ASAHI TV BUILDING

Takenaka Corporation

DESIGN ARCHITECT, HOUSING

CD Partnership

PROJECT ARCHITECT, RETAIL

Takenaka Corporation

LANDSCAPE ARCHITECT

EDAW, Inc.

STATUS

Design development

Dentsu Headquarters
at Shiodome
Tokyo, Japan

DATE

Start date 1997

Finish date 2002

PROJECT TYPE

Mixed-use

SITE AREA

185,341 s.f./17,225 m²

COMPONENTS

Corporate headquarters offices 1,850,720

   s.f./172,000 m²

Retail and restaurants 161,400 s.f./15,000 m²

Performing arts theater and entertainment

   64,560 s.f./6,000 m²

CLIENT

Obayashi Corporation

PROJECT TEAM

DESIGN CONSULTANT

The Jerde Partnership International, Inc.

DESIGN ARCHITECT, HEADQUARTERS TOWER

Architectures Jean Nouvel

EXECUTIVE ARCHITECT

Obayashi Corporation

LANDSCAPE ARCHITECT

EDAW, Inc.

WATER FEATURE DESIGNER

WET Design

STATUS

Design development

Namba
Osaka, Japan

DATE

Start date 1996

Finish date 2003

PROJECT TYPE

Mixed-use, with retail and entertainment

SITE AREA

400,000 s.f./37,179 m²

COMPONENTS

Total building area 3,195,000 s.f./297,000 m²

Commercial 1,178,000 s.f./109,500 m²

   Restaurants

   Retail

   Amusement

   Cinema

Cultural 26,900 s.f./2,500 m²

Office 1,183,000 s.f./110,000 m²

Common area 527,000 s.f./49,000 m²

Parking spaces 1,251

CLIENT

Nankai Electric Railway Co, Ltd

Obayashi Corporation

PROJECT TEAM

DESIGN CONSULTANT

The Jerde Partnership International, Inc.

PROJECT ARCHITECT

Obayashi Corporation

LANDSCAPE ARCHITECT

EDAW, Inc.

SPD Collab Inc.

LIGHTING DESIGNER

Joe Kaplan Architectural Lighting

WATER FEATURE DESIGNER

WET Design

ENVIRONMENTAL DESIGNER

Selbert Perkins Design Collaborative, Inc.

STATUS

Design development

Zlota Centre
Warsaw, Poland

DATE

Start date 1997

Finish date 2003

PROJECT TYPE

Mixed-use urban retail and entertainment

   center

SITE AREA

1,950,000 s.f./182,000 m²

COMPONENTS

Office 258,000 s.f./24,000 m²

Hotel 376,000 s.f./35,000 m²

Cinema 107,000 s.f./10,000 m²

Retail 645,000 s.f./60,000 m²

Parking 484,000 s.f./45,000 m²

CLIENT

ING Real Estate

PROJECT TEAM

DESIGN ARCHITECT

The Jerde Partnership International, Inc.

EXECUTIVE ARCHITECT

Epstein + Sons Int'l Inc.

STATUS

Design development

Firm Background

Founded in 1977 in Los Angeles, California, the Jerde Partnership International is a 130-member urban planning and architecture firm. In 1983, architect, urbanist and Jerde Partnership founder Jon Jerde was selected to conceptualize and design the 1984 Olympic Games in Los Angeles. His innovative solution received international acclaim and numerous awards. In 1985, the Jerde Partnership reinvented the retail-office-hotel complex with the opening of Horton Plaza in downtown San Diego. The $140 million project set into motion a new way of thinking about retail, downtown and suburban centers, as well as the process of bringing people together.

For twenty-two years the firm has been developing theories and methodologies to design more human-scaled projects that offer heightened experience—a design language that combines functionality with impact. The firm has developed an integrated method of working on its projects, organized around co-creative teams of collaborators, clients and consultants to create projects that benefit from the input of many sources of expertise. The firm's innovative ideas are being realized in more than 65 projects in process in Asia, Europe and North and South America. The Jerde Partnership often devises the concept or masterplan, and is then involved in coordinating the co-creative teams to carry through those ideas. During the project management and through to the design completion stages, the role played by the Jerde Partnership varies with individual projects.

The Jerde Partnership has received considerable international recognition for its projects and ideas, from organizations such as the American Institute of Architects (AIA), *Progressive Architecture* magazine, the International Council of Shopping Centers (ICSC), Urban Land Institute, *VM&SD* magazine, Bouwprijs, European ICSC, Nederlandse Raad voor Winkelcentra, Royal Australian Institute of Architects and the Japanese Ministry of International Trade and Industry.

List of Projects 1977–99

Planning projects
North America

Ahmanson Ranch, Ventura County, CA
Home Savings of America

Atlantic City Boardwalk, Atlantic City, NJ
Casino Reinvestment Development Authority

Bass Pro Site, Fort Lauderdale, FL
Belz Enterprises

Cancun Town Center, Cancun, Mexico
Plaza Caracol Dos, Sa De CV

Chula Vista Bayfront, Chula Vista, CA
Chula Vista Investors

Churchill Church Farm School, Chester County, PA
Rouse & Associates

Desert Ridge, Phoenix, AZ
Northeast Phoenix Partners

Eastlake, City of Elsinore, CA
Eastlake Community Builders

Epcot Center, Orlando, FL
Disney Development Co.

Hollywood Center, Hollywood, CA
Melvin Simon & Associates

Indian School, Phoenix, AZ
Barron Collier Company

Mission City, Mission Valley, San Diego, CA
Fenton Industries

Mission Valley, San Diego, CA
Fenton-Western Properties, Inc.

Monte Vista, Phoenix, AZ
Homefree Village Resorts, Inc.

Monticello Raceway, Monticello, NY
America's Partners

New Port City, Jersey City, NJ
Melvin Simon & Sam Le-Frak

Niagara Falls, Niagara Falls, NY
Niagara Falls Redevelopment

Penn's Landing, Philadelphia, PA
Rouse & Associates

Rancho La Sierra, Riverside, CA
Rancho La Sierra Partnership

Riverfront Center, Hartford, CT
The Mead Group

Queen's Bay, Long Beach, CA
Wrather Corporation

Santa Fe Town Center, Mexico City, Mexico
Reichmann International L.P.
ICA-Reichmann Santa Fe SA de CV
ICA

Scripps Ranch, San Diego County, CA
McMillan Properties

Shoreline Park, Long Beach, CA
Ratkovich Group

Soulanges Canal, Soulanges Canal, Canada
The Courrough Consulting Group

Sunterra, Palm Desert, CA
Sunrise Development Co.

Trancas Canyon Community, Malibu, CA
RECO Land Corporation

Universal City Masterplan, Universal City, CA
MCA Development Co.

Asia

Al Shuwaikh, Sea City, Kuwait
Kuwait Real Estate Group

Baiyangdian Hot Springs, Beijing, China
Chairman Tang

Batam Center, Jakarta, Indonesia
PRC/Indonesia

Bundang Masterplan, Bundang, South Korea
Posco Engr. & Cons. Co., Ltd.

Chonan Hot Springs, Chonan, South Korea
Delco Consulting Group

Chung Hsiao E Road, Taipei, Taiwan
Der Jey Affiliated Organization

Daiba BT-21, Tokyo, Japan
Mitsubishi/Takenaka Corp.

Kenny Heights, Kuala Lumpur, Malaysia
Kenny Height Dev. SDN BHD

King Fahad National Park, Taif, Saudi Arabia
PRC Group

Kuwait Waterfront, Kuwait
Kuwait Real Estate Co.

Malacca Waterfront, Malaca, Malaysia
Olympia Land Berhad

MM21—Block 24, Yokohama, Japan
Takenaka/Hypercross 24 Group

Nagoya Gateway, Nagoya, Japan
International Leisure Consultant

Natori, City of Sendai, Japan
Daishowa Greenport/Obayashi

Orchard Road, Singapore
DP Architects PTE., Ltd.

Pearls of Kuwait, Kuwait
Khaled Yousef Al-Marzook

Rinku Masterplan and Town Block III, Osaka, Japan
Nihon Seimei/Sumitomo

Rosetown Masterplan, Kyoto, Japan
Obayashi Corp.

Saita, Shikoku Island, Japan
Pacific Art & Design Consultant

San Chee Housing Development, San Chee, Taiwan
Sing Tran Company

Tomakomai, Hokkaido, Japan
Daiwa House Industry Co., Ltd.

Europe

Bay of Palma, Majorca, Spain
Trizec Hahn Europe GMBH

Elysee II, Versailles, France
EuroFrance

Euro Park Mougins, Les Breguieres, France
Tor Andenaes S.A.

Harborside, Bristol, United Kingdom
John Warman/London Met. PLC

Miramer, Cannes, France
Tor Andenaes S.A.

Satellite New Town, Near Paris, France
The Jerde Partnership International

Wolfsburg, Wolfsburg, Germany
Autovision

Australia

Cuba Mall, Wellington, New Zealand
Mace Development Co.

Princess Wharf, Auckland, New Zealand
Mace Development Co.

Retail-based projects
North America

Bajamar Resort Village, Ensenada, BCN Mexico
Sunrise Development

Bellevue Center, Bellevue, WA
Wright-Runstad

Belz Orlando, Orlando, FL
Belz Enterprises

Chula Vista Center, Chula Vista, CA
Homart Development Co.

Citicorp, Los Angeles, CA
TrizecHahn Office Mgmt.

Del Mar Plaza, Del Mar, CA
Del Mar Partnership

Downtown Plaza, Sacramento, CA
The Hahn Company

Eaton Place, Eaton, Canada
Nationale—Nederlanden R.E.

Edmonton Centre, Edmonton, Canada
Oxford Properties

Farmers Market, Los Angeles, CA
Madison Marquette Realty

Fashion Island, Newport Beach, CA
Irvine Retail Properties

Glendale Galleria, Glendale, CA
Donahue-Schriber

Horton Plaza, San Diego, CA
The Hahn Company

La Cumbre Plaza, Santa Barbara, CA
The Hahn Company

Los Cerritos Center, Cerritos, CA
The Hahn Company

Main Place/Santa Ana, Orange Country, CA
Santa Ana Venture

Mall of America, Bloomington, MN
Melvin Simon & Associates

Marina Mazatlan Resort Village, Mazatlan, SIN Mexico
Sunrise Development

Metro Town Square, Vancouver, BC, Canada
Trilea Centers, Inc.

Montclair Plaza, Montclair, CA
Homart Development Co.

Moreno Valley at Towngate, Moreno Valley, CA
Homart Development Co.

North County Fair, Escondido, CA
The Hahn Company

Prestonwood, Dallas, TX
TrizecHahn Centers

Sam Goody—Horton Plaza, San Diego, California
Sam Goody

Sam Goody—Universal CityWalk, Universal City, CA
Sam Goody

Seventh Street Marketplace, Los Angeles, CA
Oxford Properties/Prudential+

Sports Planet, Torrance, CA
Pacific Art and Design

The Courtyard, Rolling Hills Estate, CA
The Hahn Company

The Pavilion, San Jose, CA
Melvin Simon & Kimball Small

The Shops at Palos Verdes, Palos Verdes, CA
The Shops at Palos Verdes

The Village at Corte Madera, Corte Madera, CA
The Hahn Company

Topanga Plaza, Canoga Park, CA
May Centers

University Towne Centre, San Diego, CA
TrizecHahn Centers Mgmt. Inc.

Vail Valley Center, Vail, CO
End Limited Liability

Vancouver—Downtown Site, Vancouver, BC Canada
Trilea Centers, Inc.

Westside Pavilion and Expansion, Los Angeles, CA
Westfield Inc.

South America

Paseo Alcorta, Buenos Aires, Argentina
New Shopping S.A.

Asia

Balikpapan Center, Balikpapan, Indonesia
P.T. Pandega Citraniaga

Chia Tai Riverfest, Shanghai, China
Shanghai-Kinghill Ltd.

Core Pacific City, Taipei, Taiwan
Core Pacific

Fukuchiyama, Fukuchiyama, Japan
Obayashi Corporation

Greenhill, Kuwana, Japan
ANQ, Nichii Co., Obayashi

Ibaraki Project, Ibaraki, Japan
Mycal General Dev. Co., Ltd.

Lippovillage Supermall, Jakarta, Indonesia
Lippo Group

Makuhari Town Center, Chiba, Japan
Mitsubishi

MetroWalk, Taipei, Taiwan
D.C. International Co., Ltd.

Oita Town Center, Oita, Japan
Fukuoka Japan, Urban Design

Pacific Century Place, Beijing, China
Pacific Century Group

Sakae Park, Nagoya, Japan
Obayashi Corp.

Sudirman Retail Center, Jakarta, Indonesia
John Portman & Associates

The Peak Galleria, Victoria Peak, Hong Kong
Hang Lung Development Co.

Tian He Grandview Plaza, Guangzhou, China

Chia Tai Group

Tian Jin Downtown Plaza, Tian Jin, China
Tianjin Datian Real Estate Dev.

Europe

Beursplein, Rotterdam, The Netherlands
Multi Vastgoed b.v.

Australia

Chatswood Shopping Town Centre, Sydney, Australia
Westfield, Inc.

Robina Town Centre, Queensland, Australia
Robina Land Corp. Pty., Ltd.

Rotorua Specialty Center, Rotorua, New Zealand
Retail Construction. Ltd.

Mixed-use projects
North America

Bellevue Entertainment Complex, Bellevue, WA
E&H Investments

Block 113 Mixed-Use, Long Beach, CA
Long Beach Dev. Agency

Circle Center, Indianapolis, IN
Melvin Simon & Associates

Collier Center, Phoenix, AZ
Barron Collier Company

Emeryville Retail Project, Emeryville, CA
Madison Marquette Realty

Exposition Park/Coliseum, Los Angeles, CA
Community Redev. Agency

Glendale Town Center, Glendale, CA
Donahue Schriber

Hollywood Marketplace, Hollywood, CA
Regent Properties

Kansas City Power and Light District, Kansas City, MO
Centertainment Power & Light

Keeaumoku/Ohai Plaza, Honolulu, HI
Haseko

Marina Place, Culver City, CA
Melvin Simon & Associates

Market Place, Austin, TX
Lamar Sixth Austin, Inc.

Meadowlands Sports Complex, New Jersey, NJ
LCOR

Outrigger—Waikiki, Honolulu, HI
Forest City Development

Pointe Anaheim Dev. Project, Anaheim, CA
Western Asset Mgmt.

Stratton, Stratton, VT
Intrawest Resorts

The Gateway, Salt Lake City, UT
Boyer Company

The Pageant on Hennepin Avenue, Minneapolis, MN
Ray Harris Company

Universal CityWalk, Universal City, CA
MCA Development Co.

Universal CityWalk Expansion, Universal City, CA
Universal Creative

Yerba Buena, San Francisco, CA
Olympia & York

South America

Argentina Retail Entertainment, Bahia Blanca, Argentina
Grainco, S.A.

Argentina Retail Entertainment, San Justo, Argentina
Grainco, S.A.

Argentina Retail Entertainment, Santa Fe, Argentina
Grainco, S.A.

Asia

Awaji Laguna Village, Osaka, Japan
Awaji Island Resort Dev. Group

BR-4 Retail/Entertainment Project, Taipei, Taiwan
Forest City Development

Canal City Hakata, Fukuoka, Japan
Sumitomo Life Insurance Company
Fukuoka Jisho Co., Ltd.
Fukuoka Japan, Urban Design and Development Co., Ltd.

Central Pattana/Chonburi, Bangkok, Thailand
Central Pattana Public Co., Ltd.

Conrad Interior Plaza, Jakarta, Indonesia
Pt. Arthayasa Grahatama

Daiba Tokyo Broadway, Daiba, Japan
Mitsubishi

Daikan Home Ise Shima Resort, Mie Prefecture, Japan
Daikan Home/Funakoshi Onsen

Dalian Mixed-Use, Dalian, China
Eton Properties, Ltd.

Dentsu Headquarters at Shiodome, Tokyo, Japan
Obayashi Corporation

Hyundai Mok-Dong, Seoul, Korea
Keum Kang Dev. Industrial Co.

Kangwan Casino Resort, Seoul, Korea
SAC International, Ltd.

Kishiwada Port, Kishiwada, Japan
Kishiwada Port Authority

Kitakyushu, Kitakyushu, Japan
Fukuoka Japan, Urban Design and Development Co., Ltd.

Kobe Newport Island, Kobe, Japan
Osaka Gas

Kolin Redevelopment, Taipei, Taiwan
Fukuoka Japan, Urban Design and Development Co., Ltd.

Lippo Plaza—Beijing, Beijing, China
Lippo Group

Marina 21—Daewoo, Seoul, Korea
Daewoo Corporation

MCA—Osaka, Osaka, Japan
Universal Creative

Middle East Waterfront, Middle East
Kuwait Real Estate Group

Namba, Osaka, Japan
Obayashi Corporation

Nanjing Zilu Redevelopment, Shanghai, China
Hang Lung Development Co.

Nations Wealth Plaza, Beijing, China
Pacific Century

North Triangle, Manila, Philippines
Fil-Estate

Okinawa, Okinawa, Japan
The Daiei, Inc.

Otaru Bay, Otaru, Japan
Mycar General Development

Rama 9, Bangkok, Thailand
Central Pattana Nine Square

Rokko Island, Kobe, Japan
Daiwa House Industry Co., Ltd.

Roppongi 6-6, Tokyo, Japan
Mori Building Company, Ltd.

Samsung Experience, Seoul, Korea
Samoo Architects

Shinagawa Mixed-Use, Shinagawa, Japan
Fukuoka Japan, Urban Design and Development Co., Ltd.

Southwoods Ecocentrum, Manila, Philippines
Fil-Estate

Sudirman Central Business District, Jakarta, Indonesia
Jakarta Intl. Hotel & Dev.

Tai chung, Taipei, Taiwan
BES Engineering Corporation

Tel Aviv Mixed-Use, Tel Aviv, Israel
Drive-In Cinema T.A.. Ltd.

Tokyo Mills, Tokyo, Japan
Mills Management, LLC

Europe

Croydon Gateway, Croydon, UK
Land Securities PLC

One Reeperbahn, Hamburg, Germany
Gedusham Properties

Spuimarket, The Hague, Holland
Multi Vesti 87 b.v.

West End City Center, Budapest, Hungary
Triganit Development Corp.

Zlota Centre, Warsaw, Poland
ING Real Estate

Africa

Mall of Egypt, Cairo, Egypt
Famco Dev. Group

Entertainment projects
North America

Los Angeles Olympic Games, Los Angeles, CA
LA Olympic Organizing Committee

AMC/Deer Valley, Phoenix, AZ
American Multi-Cinema

AMC 20- & 24-Plex Prototype
American Multi-Cinema

Atlantic City Le Jardin, Atlantic City, NJ

Mirage Resorts, Inc.
Blockbuster Park, Miami, FL
  Blockbuster
Bridgeport Sporting Club, Bridgeport, CT
  Mirage Resorts, Inc.
Casino Royale, New Orleans, LA
  Mirage Resorts, Inc.
Centennial Sports Complex, Nashville, TN
  City of Nashville & T. Miller
Cinetropolis—Woodfield Mall, Schaumburg, IL
  IWERKS
Culver City Entertainment, Culver City, CA
  Caplow and Associate, Inc.
Detroit Casino, Detroit, MI
  Mirage Resorts, Inc.
The Fremont Street Experience, Las Vegas, NV
  Fremont Street Experience Limited Liability
  Company
GameWorks Seattle, Seattle, WA
  Sega GameWorks, LLC
GameWorks Las Vegas, Las Vegas, NV
  Sega GameWorks, LLC
GameWorks Ontario, Ontario, CA
  Sega GameWorks, LLC
Hollywood Park, Los Angeles, CA
  Koll Real Estate Group
Luminaire, Houston, TX
  Skywalker Development
MCAR—Florida, Orlando, FL
  MCA Development Co.
Metropolis Times Square, New York, NY
  Broadway State Partners
Millenia Walk, Singapore
  Pontiac Marina
Mud Island, Memphis, TN
  Pyramid Operating Authority
Peabody Place, Memphis, TN
  Belz Enterprises
Pyramid, Memphis, TN
  Pyramid Group
Santa Anita Entertainment Center, Arcadia, CA
  The Hahn Company
Scottsdale Sportsplex, Scottsdale, AZ
  Gordon Company
Skydome, Toronto, Canada
  Cogan Capital Group
Spectrum Anaheim, Anaheim, CA
  Y & M Incorporated
Sportstown Anaheim, Anaheim, CA
  Forest City Development, Co.
Treasure Island, Las Vegas, NV
  Mirage Resorts, Inc.
Urbanopolis, Anaheim, CA
  Disney Development Co.

South America
Buenos Aires Casino, Buenos Aires, Argentina
  Mirage Resorts, Inc.

Asia
Cinecitta, Kawasaki, Japan
  Kawasaki Misu Co., Ltd.

Hirakata Park, Osaka, Japan
  Kai Kikaku, Inc.
Osaka Dome, Osaka, Japan
  Obayashi Corp.
Osaka—Universal Gateway, Osaka, Japan
  Universal Creative

Europe
Sakalidis Mega-plex, Athens, Greece
  Village Roadshow Greece, S.A.
Star City, Birmingham, UK
  Tarmac Development Mgmt
Utrecht Entertainment Project, Utrecht,
  The Netherlands
  Multi Vastgoed b.v.

Africa
Sun International—Capetown, Capetown,
  South Africa
  Sun International

Commercial office projects
North America
Bedford Drive, Beverly Hills, CA
  DMG, Ltd.
Gateway Center, Colorado Springs, CO
  Carver Development
Tatung Office and Warehouse, San Diego, CA
  Tatung Company of America
The Power Plant, Baltimore, MD
  Six Flags
Trizec Office Building, Kansas City, MO
  Trizec Inc.

Asia
Samsung Headquarters, Seoul, Korea
  Samsung Engr. & Cons. Co. Ltd.

Hotel Projects
North America
Adolphis Hotel, Dallas, TX
  Westgroup Inc.
Bellagio, Las Vegas, NV
  Mirage Resorts, Inc.
Hotel Paso del Norte, El Paso, TX
  Franklin Land Company

Asia
Grand Hyatt Fukuoka, Fukuoka, Japan
  Fukuoka Jisho Company
Washington Hotel, Fukuoka, Japan
  Fukuoka Jisho Company

Institutional projects
North America
Children's Museum, Los Angeles, CA
  LA Children's Museum
Doolittle Theater, Los Angeles, CA
  Regent Properties
Fashion Institute of Design and Merchandising,
  Los Angeles, CA
  FIDM Realty Corporation

Fireman's Memorial, Sacramento, CA
  CA Fire Foundation

Renovation/Re-use projects
North America
405, 416 and 450 North Bedford Drive, Beverly
  Hills, CA
  DMG, Ltd.
435 and 436 Roxbury Drive, Beverly Hills, CA
  DMG, Ltd.
1001 Gayley Avenue Office Building,
  Westwood, CA
  DMG, Ltd.
Exchange Building, Seattle, WA
  Pacific Seaboard Group
Fix-Madore Building, Seattle, WA
  Elliot Bay Associates
Seventh and Hope Building, Los Angeles, CA
  Westgroup Inc.

Africa
Sphinx Preservation, Giza, Egypt
  AERA, Inc.

Selected Awards
(Others listed in project data)
Sam Goody, Universal City, California, Design
  Award, *VM&SD* magazine, 1994
Ise Shima Resort, Mie Prefecture, Japan,
  Urban Design Citation, *Progressive
  Architecture* magazine, 1991
Bronze Award for Architectural Excellence,
  Stucco Manufacturers Association, 1989
Certificate of National Merit, US Department of
  Housing and Urban Development, 1986
The Power Plant, Baltimore, Maryland
  Citation, AIA, Los Angeles chapter, 1983
Adolphus Hotel, Dallas, Texas
  Design Award, AIA, Dallas chapter, 1982

Biography

Jon Adams Jerde FAIA

1940 Born in Alton, Illinois

Spends childhood in New Orleans; various towns in Texas; St. Paul, Minnesota; and various towns in Idaho

1952 Moves to Southern California

1957–58 Studies art and engineering at the University of California at Los Angeles (UCLA)

1959–65 Transfers to the University of Southern California (USC) and graduates from the School of Architecture with a Bachelor of Architecture degree

1963 Awarded a Traveling Fellowship from the USC Architecture Guild

Travels to Europe where the Greek Islands and Tuscany's hill towns become a life-long inspiration

1964 Awarded the Henry Clay Gold Medal for outstanding student work from the American Institute of Architects (AIA)

1964 Joins Dworsky Associates, Inc.

Awarded a *Progressive Architecture* magazine design award for the design of the UCLA football stadium

1965–66 Forms Jerde Aleksich with partner John Aleksich

1967–77 Becomes director of design at Burke, Kober, Nicholais, Archuleta, later to become Charles Kober Associates, one of Southern California's largest shopping center design firms

Develops a set of ideas that emphasizes the importance of communal space. Attempts to transform shopping malls into venues for communal activity

1977 Leaves Charles Kober Associates because of the retail industry's resistance to new ideas about transforming these "consumption machines"

Renovates historic structures in Los Angeles and Seattle

Founds The Jerde Partnership when developer Ernest Hahn gives him the opportunity to apply his ideas about communal space to the design of a new, large-scale shopping district, Horton Plaza, in abandoned downtown San Diego

1982 Selected as design director for the 1984 Los Angeles Olympic Games to lead the core team of designers and artists

1983 Establishes the Urban Design Advisory Coalition (UDAC), a group of Southern California architects, designers, urban planners, artists and writers who explore solutions for the urban problems of Los Angeles and the Southern California region

1985 Receives the Distinguished Alumnus Award, School of Architecture, USC

1987 Appointed to Los Angeles Mayor Tom Bradley's Design Advisory Coalition as one of six professionals who advise him on design issues related to the city

1988 Receives the Mayor's Certificate of appreciation from the City of Los Angeles for his contributions to the Mayor's Design Advisory Coalition.

1990 Elected to the College of Fellows, AIA

1991 Receives *Progressive Architecture* magazine's Urban Design Citation for Ise Shima Resort, Mie Prefecture, Japan

1992 Receives the Golden Plate Award from the American Academy of Achievement

1992 Becomes a founding member, Ancient Egypt Research Associates, organized to assist the Semitic Institute of Harvard University with the conservation of the Giza plateau in Egypt

1997 Becomes the first recipient of the Los Angeles AIA chapter's Pacific Rim Award for design excellence in projects in Asia

1998 The Jerde Partnership's Canal City Hakata project selected for the international traveling exhibition, *At the End of the Century: One Hundred Years of Architecture*, organized by the Museum of Contemporary Art (MOCA), Los Angeles

1987–99 Teaches design at various colleges and universities including UCLA, USC, Harvard University Graduate School of Design Professional Development Courses, and Southern California Institute of Architecture (SCI–Arc)

Professional and Community Affiliations

Member, College of Fellows, American Institute of Architects (AIA)

Founding Member, Ancient Egypt Research Associates

Member, Greater Los Angeles Zoo Association

Patron, Hollywood Bowl

Member, International Council of Shopping Centers (ICSC)

Patron Member, Modern and Contemporary Art Council (MCAC), Los Angeles County Museum of Art (LACMA)

Artist's Circle Member, Los Angeles Opera

Member, Director's Forum, The Museum of Contemporary Art (MOCA), Los Angeles

Member, National Council of Architectural Registration Boards (NCARB)

Corporate Associate, University of San Diego

Member, Urban Design Advisory Coalition (UDAC), City of Los Angeles

Associate, Urban Land Institute (ULI)

Member, Venice (California) Chamber of Commerce

Member, Board of Directors, Yo San University

Select Bibliography
Books and Books in Progress

Jerde, Jon, with Stephanie Smith, *Jon Jerde: His Vision and Ideas* (2000)

Gandel, Cathie, *Jon Jerde and the Making of Canal City Hakata* (Los Angeles: Balcony Press, 2000)

Boomkens, René, *A Threshold World* (Rotterdam: Netherlands Architecture Institute, 1999)

Moore, Rowan, *Vertigo* (London: Calmann and King Publishers, 1999)

Uddin, Mohammed Saleh, *Digital Architecture* (New York: McGraw-Hill, 1999)

Dixon, John Morris, ed., *Urban Spaces* (New York: Retail Reporting, 1999)

Pegler, Martin M., *Entertainment: Places and Spaces* (New York: Retail Reporting, Urban Land Institute, 1999)

Architectural Profiles of Small Shopping Centers: Del Mar Plaza, Del Mar, California (New York: International Council of Shopping Centers, ICSC, 1999)

The Jerde Partnership International: Visceral Reality (Milan: L'Arca Edizioni, 1999)

Pearman, Hugh, *Contemporary World Architecture* (London: Phaidon Press, 1998)

Ibelings, Hans, *Supermodernism: The Architecture in the Age of Globalization* (Rotterdam: NAI Publishers, 1998)

Poulin, L. Richard, *Image, Type, Architecture: A History of Environmental Graphic Design* (New York: Van Nostrand Reinhold, 1998), featuring the Fremont Street Experience, Las Vegas

Markham, Julian E., *The Future of Shopping—Traditional Patterns and the Net Effects* (London: MacMillan, 1998)

Urban Entertainment Graphics (New York: Madison Square Press, 1997): Jon Jerde, "Capturing the Zeitgeist," pp. 10–13. Wayne Hunt, "Overhead Drama: The Fremont Street Experience," pp. 52–54

Canal City Hakata Concept Book (Fukuoka, Japan: Urban Design & Development Co., 1997)

Huxtable, Ada Louise, *The Unreal America: Architecture and Illusion* (New York: The New Press, 1997)

Ghirardo, Diane, *Architecture after Modernism* (London: Thames & Hudson, 1997), featuring Westside Pavilion, Los Angeles, pp. 65, 214 and 230

Taguchi, Yasushiko, and I. M. Tao, *American Shopping Centers 2* (Japan: Books Nippan, 1996), featuring Universal CityWalk, Los Angeles, pp. 9–16, and Downtown Plaza, Sacramento, pp. 17–24

Kirkpatrick, Grant Camden, *Shops and Boutiques* (New York: PBC International, 1995), featuring Sam Goody and Universal CityWalk, Los Angeles, pp. 20–23

International Architecture Yearbook, volume 1, book 1 (Australia: Images Australia Ptn Ltd., 1995), featuring Peak Galleria, Hong Kong and Downtown Plaza, Sacramento, pp. 224–29

Salb, Joan G., *Retail Image & Graphic Identity* (Retail Reporting Corp., 1995), featuring Downtown Plaza, Sacramento, pp. 62–63, and Universal CityWalk, Los Angeles, pp. 74–75

Adler, Jerry, *High Rise* (London: Harper Collins, 1993), featuring Metropolis Times Square, New York

Jencks, Charles, *Heteropolis* (London: Academy Editions, 1993), featuring Universal CityWalk, Los Angeles, pp. 46–48

Frieden, Bernard J., and Lynne B. Sagalyn, *Downtown, Inc.: How America Rebuilds Cities* (Cambridge: The MIT Press, 1989), featuring Horton Plaza, San Diego

Selected Articles
1998

Bergsman, Steve, "A $500 Million Mixed Project for Phoenix," *The New York Times*, December 20, p. 61

Silver, Allison, "Jon Jerde: Pioneering Architect Who Put 'Experience' into Downtowns," *Los Angeles Times*, December 20, p. M3

Anderton, Frances, "The Maker of Today's Cathedrals," *The San Diego Union Tribune*, November 8, pp. H1, H4

Anderton, Frances, "The Global Village Goes to Pop Baroque," *The New York Times*, October 8, pp. F1, F7

"New Forms of Community: Horton Plaza, Beursplein, Core Pacific City," *Dialogue*, July, pp. 20–37

Bergren, Ann, "Jon Jerde's Architecture of Pleasure," *Daidalos*, June, pp. 60–67

Pearson, Clifford, "American Institute of Architects 1998 Honors & Awards," *Architectural Record*, May, p. 124

Rickards, Jane, "Core Pacific Breaks Ground on Metro-mall," *China News*, March 9, p. 7

"King Hwa Shopping Center," *Space*, March, Korea, pp. 41–51

Miller, Robert, "Narrative Urban Landscapes," *Urban Land*, February, pp. 62–65, 92

1997

"Asia's Best Cities," *AsiaWeek*, December 5

Daly, James, "Architecture as Entertainment," *Wired*, November, p. 213

Gandel, Cathie, "Canal City Hakata: An American Concept Blossoms in Japan," *The American Chamber of Commerce in Japan Journal*, November, pp. 44–49

"Business News," *The Daily Telegraph*, September 15, p. 26

"Urban Development: Even Mahathir was Impressed," *AsiaWeek*, September 12, p. 50

Davis, Jim, "Power & Light Designers Seek Community," *Kansas City Business Journal*, August 29–September 4, pp. 3, 46

"Bahía de shopping," *Ingenier & Arquitectura*, August 19, p. 1

Helliker, Kevin, "Theater Mogul Tries to Bring Kansas City Up to Date," *Wall Street Journal*, August 6, pp. B1, B6

Brandenberg, Mark, "The Fremont Street Experience: Revitalizing Downtown," *Communique*, August, pp. 19, 27

Scott, Cathy, "Lights! Sound! Action!," *Los Angeles Times*, July 16, pp. 5, 15

Fukuda, Masako, "Swath of Color Paints Bold Path for Retailers," *The Nikkei Weekly*, July 7, pp. 1, 21

Weatherford, Mike, "Changing Faces of Las Vegas," *Las Vegas Review-Journal*, July 6, pp. 1A, 8A

"Making Places," *World Architecture*, July–August

Moore, Jonathan, "Reports from the Pacific Rim: Taiwan," *Architectural Record*, July, p. 84

Moustafa, Amer A., and James M. Forsher, "Reinventing the Mall: A Conversation with Jon Jerde," *Lusk Review*, Summer, pp. 31–39

Burman, Tsilah, and Cheri Brown, "Entertainment Centers: A Creative Approach," *California Centers*, Spring, p. 32

"Developers See the Light," *Kansas City Business Journal*, April 18

Rybczynski, Witold, "The Pasteboard Past: Historic Preservation, Ada Louise Huxtable Argues, Is Not Always a Good Thing," *The News York Times Book Review*, April 6, p. 13

Huxtable, Ada Louise, "Living with the Fake and Liking It," *The New York Times*, March 30, Section 2, pp. 1, 40

Sullivan, Kristina B., "Case Study: A 10/100M-bps Ethernet Network Pipes New Life into Cities," *PC Week*, March 3, pp. 81, 96

Stein, Karen, "Canal City Hakata, Fukuoka, Japan," *Architectural Record*, March, pp. 110–15

"Time, the Universe and Everything," *VM&SD*, February, p. 11

1996

"Jon Jerde," *Los Angeles Magazine*, December, p. 118

"Learning to Walk in Las Vegas," *Architect's Journal*, October 10, p. 26

Van Bossum, Bernard, "Winkelen onder de grond: Beursplein Rotterdam op jacht naar 2,3 miljoen klanter," *Algemeen Daglad*, August 31, The Netherlands

Iritani, Evelyn, "A Mall Master Takes on the World," *Los Angeles Times*, July 5, pp. 1, A17

Showley, Roger, "It All Began Here," *The San Diego Union Tribune*, June 9, pp. H2, H4

Shimokawa, Kazuya, "Canal City Hakata," *Nikkei Design*, June, pp. 46–54

"A Canal Runs Through It," *The Japan Times*, April 17

Cashill, Robert, "Lighting Las Vegas" and "Downtown Las Vegas Hits the Jackpot with a One-of-a-kind Light-and-Sound Spectacular," *Lighting Dimensions*, April, pp. 58–61, 97–99

Anderton, Frances, "The Wow Factor," *Blueprint*, April, pp. 40–43

"Fremont Street Experience," *Architecture*, April, pp. 88–89

Newman, Morris, "What Happens to a Street when it Becomes an Experience?," *Metropolis*, April, pp. 23, 26

Webb, Michael, "The Glitter and the Grit," *Los Angeles Times*, March 24, pp. M1, M3

Skalsky, Judi, trans. Renguan Zhao, "Special Issue: The Jerde Partnership and Experiential Design," *Time + Architecture*, China, February, pp. 1–13

Barr, Vilma, "Sam Goody's got it," *Retail Store Image*, January, pp. 22–28

1995

Gorman, Tom, "It's lights, action, excess in Las Vegas," *Los Angeles Times*, December 2, pp. 1, A24

Sloan, David, Tridib Banerjee, Genevieve Guiliano, Greg Hise, "Invented Streets: New Retail Formats," *Research Report No. LCRI-9601R*, Lusk Center Research Institute—USC School of Urban and Regional Planning, November

Fader, Steven, "Universal CityWalk," *Urban Entertainment Destinations*, August, pp. 18–19, 22–23

Hernandez, Greg, "CityWalk designer to develop a version of Anaheim Stadium area," *Los Angeles Times*, February 25, p. A10

1994

Clafton, Sara, "CFM, Robina to develop $350M shopping centre," *Australian*, October 11

Calistro, Paddy, "Jerde unplugged," *Los Angeles Magazine*, October, pp. 72–76

Latham, Aaron, "Walking the walk in LA," *The New York Times*, September, pp. 12, 27

Rubin, Michael S., Robert J. Gorman, Michael H. Lawry, "Entertainment returns to Gotham," *Urban Land Institute*, August, pp. 59–65

Richmond, Holly L., "Come one, come mall," *Contract Design*, July, pp. 52–55

Wharton, David, "A Walk on the Mild Side," *Los Angeles Times—Valley Edition*, May 27, pp. 10–11, 35

Kamin, Blair, "Three attempts to marry form

and feeling," *Chicago Tribune*, May 15

Beckett, Andy, "CityWalk: Zoo di Architecture," *Arbitare*, May, pp. 258–61

Radulski, John P., "Swashbuckling pirates make a splash at an adventurously designed casino resort," *Hospitality Design*, May, pp. 42–47

Bierman, M. Lindsay, "CityWalk's public pretensions," *Architecture*, April, p. 41

Accinelli, Laura, "Vegas hotel strikes it rich with Treasure Island idea," *Washington Sunday Times*, February 13

Delsohn, Gary, "A troubling model of hope," *The Sacramento Bee*, January 9, pp. H1, H2

1993

Betsky, Aaron, "Future World," *Los Angeles Times Magazine*, December 12, pp. 41–5, 52

Gorman, Tom, "High Stakes Style," *Los Angeles Times Magazine*, December 12, pp. 46–52

Wood, Daniel B., "LA's CityWalk puts people back on the street," *The Christian Science Monitor*, December 7, p. 12

Whiteson, Leon, "Dream Street," *Los Angeles Times*, October 31, pp. K1, K7

Peters, Matt, "Downtown Plaza: Plenty of food, entertainment, shops, razzle-dazzle," *The Sacramento Bee*, October 21, p. 4

Klein, Norman M., "A glittery bit of urban make-believe," *Los Angeles Times*, July 18

Gollner, Phillip M., "Los Angeles, the Mall," *San Francisco Examiner*, July 18

Bibisi, Suzzan, "Universal Studios theme park has become a blockbuster," *Chicago Tribune*, July 4

Gollner, Phillip M. "Mall that imitates life," *The New York Times*, June 27

Howard, T. J., "Retail strategy gets facelift," *Chicago Tribune*, May 30, pp. 1B-2B

Kahlenberg, Richard, "The city on the hill," *Los Angeles Times*, May 23, p. B15

De Turenne, Veronique, "CityWalk: Respite from an urban jungle," *Daily News*, April 6, pp. 5–6

Pearson, Clifford A., "Reworking the mall," *Architectural Record*, March, pp. 84–5

Karasov, Deborah, and Judith A. Martin, "The Mall of them all," *Design Quarterly*, Spring, pp. 18–27

Whiteson, Leon, "LA Architecture: Trashy Sophistication?," *Los Angeles Times*, February 14, pp. K2, K6

Spiller, Nancy, "There's no there here, either," *Mother Jones*, January/February, p. 14

1992

Jerde, Jon, "Instant City," *Architecture Plus*, December, p. 69

Wright, Bruce N., "It's a mall world after all," *Inland Architect*, November/December, pp. 44–49

Wright, Bruce N., "Mega mall opens in Minnesota," *Progressive Architecture*, October

"Giant mall reaches beyond retail," *Architecture*, September, p. 28

"Special Report: CAD," *AT Architecture Magazine*, Japan, September

Krier, Beth Ann, "Still a mall, mall world?," *Los Angeles Times*, August 28, pp. B10–B11

Woutat, Donald, "Ultimate challenge awaits shop-till-you-drop crowd," *Los Angeles Times*, July 27, pp. A1, A16

Davidson, John, "Prophet of the mall," *Buzz Magazine*, July–August, pp. 68–73, 94

Blair, Tom, "Downtown San Diego's amazing renaissance," *Real Estate Forum*, July, pp. 90–92

"Instant History," *Landscape Architecture*, July, p. 22

Walker, S. Lynne, "Hahn plans face lift for mall," *San Diego Union Tribune*, May 17, pp. 11–13

Mays, Vernon, "Entertainment Design: Experience over form," *Architecture*, May, pp. 95–96

"Creating an Urban Center," *In Form*, volume 4, no. 1, Spring

"Real Estate," *The Outlook*, February 5

Schwartz, Bonnie, "Neon Totems," *Interiors*, February, p. 16

1991

"The 1991 ULI Awards for Excellence: Del Mar Plaza," *Urban Land*, December, p. 17

Betsky, Aaron, "Westside Pavilion: Old-style mall turned into an assault on senses," *Los Angeles Times*, November 21, p. J2

McCloud, John, "All the mall's a stage, to retail architects," *California Real Estate Journal*, October 31, p. 16

Moosbrugger, Ed. "Leased they can do," *Santa Monica Outlook*, October 9

"When old and new mix like oil and water," *Los Angeles Times*, October 3, pp E1, E9

Fikes, Bradley J., and Laura Kaufman, "Southern Exposure," *San Diego Business Journal*, September 16, pp. A1–A4, A6–A7, A18–A19

Lowe, Jennifer, "Shopped Out," *Orange County Register*, August 12, pp. 1–2

"Architects give people priority," *Robina Review*, August, p. 3

Sklarek, Norma, "Contemporary Details: a sampler," *Architectural Review*, February, pp. 44–5

"Chula Vista project: City at a crossroads," *Los Angeles Times*, January 10, pp. E1–E2

"Ise Shima Resort," *Progressive Architecture*, January

1990

"The Westside Pavilion caters to pure shopper," *Los Angeles Times*, December 27

Seal, Mark, "The last temptation of Isaac Tigrett," *American Way—American Airlines*, November 1, pp. 70–6, 142–6

Golding, Arthur, "LA's latest buildings: Real architecture or just scenography?" *LA Architect*, September, pp. 3–4, 9

Fillip, Janice, "Improved K Street mall to boost downtown renaissance," *Sacramento Union*, August 19

McCombs, Dave, "Fanciful new headquarters for a bastion of fashion," *Los Angeles Downtown News*, August 6, pp. A1, A10, A13

Core, Richard, "Plaza grows up," *San Diego Union Tribune*, August 4, pp. B1–B2

Ivy, Robert A., "Water and Ice," *Architecture*, August, pp. 76–9

MacNeil, V., "Universal Studios gets hip in creating promenade," *Los Angeles Business Journal*, July 23, p. 40

"AIA names 4 to College of Fellows," *Los Angeles Times*, July 1

Delsohn, Gary, "Horton Plaza: People like it and use it, says Whyte," *Southern California Real Estate Journal*, June 30, p. 9

Delsohn, Gary, "Urban designers put 'heart' back into cities," *Encinitas Blade–Citizen*, June 15

"Custom response spurs refinement," *Shopping Center World*, May, pp. 292, 298

"A Blooming Orchid," *Shopping Center World*, May

Whiteson, Leon, "Universal's Urbanopolis," *Los Angeles Times*, April 15, pp. K1, K10

"Fashion Update," *Architectural Record*, April, pp. 98, 101

Haddix-Niemiec, Denise, "Script for development," *Business Daily News*, March 18

"A 90 trillion Yen development of hotels, etc.—5 groups of facilities—redevelopment of Kanebo land finalized," *Nihon Kenzai Shimbun*, March 1

"Project rises on Mel Simon's doorstep," *China Store Age Executive*, March, p. 32

Stemfel, Michael, "MCA to break ground for new shopping street," *Los Angeles Business Journal*, January 15–21, pp. 1, 14

Whiteson, Leon, "Don't forget the people, architect urges," *The Sacramento Bee*, January 14, pp. I1, I4

"Best of the Decade: 1984 Olympics," *Time*, January, p. 103

1989

Miller, Doug, and Pat Rosen, "Green light near for Luminaire?," *Houston Business Journal*, December 25, pp. 1, 10

Clifford, Frank, "LA's past may be part of its future," *Los Angeles Times*, December 25, pp. A1, A38–39

Bryant, Kathy, "An island for all seasons," *Orange County Magazine*, December, pp. 79–81

Lawrence, Herb, "Orchids and onions: Tale of two citations," *San Diego Union*, November 10

"Jon Jerde's Metropolis Times Square," *Angeles*, November, p. 34

Oltem, Carol, "Its art, commerce in Del Mar," *San Diego Union*, April 23

Taylor, Joan, "Horton Plaza designers are happy with results," *San Diego Union*, March 12

Taylor, Joan, "What can you say about Whiz Bang? Intelligent light," *San Diego Union*, March 12

Fulman, Ricki, "Times Square Whiz a Bang," *The New York Times*, February 24

Dunlap, David W., "Designer to evoke memories of Times Square in a new mall," *The New York Times*, February 24

1988

Dillon, David, "Shopping for a downtown mall," *The Dallas Morning News*, December 4, pp. 1C, 9C

Wolfle, Gretchen, "House of wood and stone," *Home and Garden*, November, pp. 46–53

Reichert, Kent, "Waterfront poses an architectural challenge," *Philadelphia Business Journal*, October 16

Grimm, Michele and Tom, "Horton Plaza among top San Diego attractions," *Los Angeles Times*, October 2, pp. 1, 15

Walker, Rosie, "Luminaire Houston," *Houston Downtown*, September 12, p. 5

"Lucasfilms hired to give facelift to Houston arena," *Variety*, September 7

Flanagan, Josephine, "US architect Jerde likes our style," *The Australian Herald*, September 5, p. 6

Loddeke, Leslie, and Steve Friedman, "Futuristic Entertainment," *Houston Post*, September 2

Downey, Roger, "Meanwhile, Downtown," *Alaska Airlines*, July, pp. 38–39

Miller, Daryl, "Taking a walk on the artistic side," *Daily News*, April 24

Adler, Jerry, and Janet Huck, "Breaking open the mall," *Newsweek*, April 18

Whiteson, Leon, "The Westside Pavilion as Neighbor," *Los Angeles Times*, March 4

Whiteson, Leon, "This is our time," *Los Angeles Times*, January 20

Berton, Brad P., "Jerde's humanistic design approach finds devotees in Hahn, Simon," *Real Estate Times*, January 16

Weber, Larry, "Jon Jerde: Designer, 1984 Olympics, Westside Pavilion, California Plaza," *Los Angeles Magazine*, January, pp. 74–75

1986

Kaplan, Sam Hall, "So says Jon Jerde," *Los Angeles Magazine*, May 11, pp. 18–19

Goldberger, Paul, "Free wheeling fantasy in San Diego," *The New York Times*, March 19, p. 8

Sachner, Paul M., "Fun City," *Architectural Record*, March, pp. 128–35

Davis, Douglas, "Raiders of the Lost Arch," *Newsweek*, January 20, pp. 66–68

1985

Kaplan, Sam Hall, "Horton Plaza: Hope, Hype," *Los Angeles Times*, August 18, pp. 1, 11

Lindsey, Robert, "San Diego builds a village just to shop in," *The New York Times*, August 17

Cleigh, Zenia, "Slices of Europe transplanted," *San Diego Union Tribune*, August 13, pp. E1, E4

Cleigh, Zenia, "Horton Plaza's designer: the evolution of a trend-setter," *San Diego Union Tribune*, August 9

Swanson, Wayne, "Horton Plaza designer: I'm trying to reinvent the American city," *Los Angeles Times*, August 8

Whiteson, Leon, "Jon Jerde designs delight— and annoy—architectural colleagues," *Los Angeles Herald Examiner*, July 21, p. E8

"Architect Jerde to discuss new Westside Pavilion," *Los Angeles Times*, July 21

"The best design in America," *ID—1985 Annual Design Review*, July–August

"Jerde's Curve," *California Magazine*, July, pp. 69–73

Guenther, Robert, "Horton Plaza may introduce shopping centers' new look," *The Wall Street Journal*, June 26

Whiteson, Leon, "New Westside mall has uptown feel," *Los Angeles Herald Examiner*, May 26, p. E4

Lindsey, Robert, "New life for San Diego's downtown," *The New York Times*, April 27

Von Eckardt, Wolf, "User friendly winners," *Time*, January 7, pp. 104–105

Jensen, Peter, "Horton Plaza—a downtown tour de force," *PSA Magazine*, January, pp. 60–63, 103–104

1984

"Awards for Excellence," *Architecture California*, November–December

Kaplan, Sam Hall, "AIA honors 16 projects in contest," *Los Angeles Times*, October 21, pp. 1, 4

Flanagan, Barbara, "Perspectives: LA 84: A Gold for Design," *Progressive Architecture*, October

Holt, Steven, "Olympics, California Style," *ID – Magazine of International Design*, September–October, pp. 22–27

Showley, Roger, "Downtown to carry on Olympic Spirit," *San Diego Union*, August 12, pp. F8–F9

1983

Showley, Roger, "San Diego's new look," *Architecture California*, September–October, pp. 17–19

Cohn, Edie, "The Adolphus Hotel, Dallas," *Interior Design*, June, pp. 214–215, 218–221

Dillon, David, "Adolphus Hotel wins top AIA honor," *The Dallas Morning News*, April 15, pp. 1C, 12C

1979

"The Jerde Partnership offices," *Arbitare*, November

Lectures and speeches
Jon Adams Jerde, FAIA

1999

"Designing Multi-use Communal Places Worldwide," Harvard University, Graduate School of Design, Cambridge, MA, USA

"Jon Jerde," Masters Lecture Series, San Diego Museum of Art, San Diego, CA, USA

"Third Spaces: Asian Manifestations," panel discussion at the fifth Harvard Asia Pacific Design conference, Harvard University, Graduate School of Design, Cambridge, MA, USA

"Satisfying the design requirements for leisure schemes," Leisure Property in Europe conference, International Quality & Productivity Centre, London, UK

"Visceral Reality," University of Southern California, Los Angeles, CA, USA

"Entertainment: The Bottom Line, a panel discussion," International Council of Shopping Centers, Whistler, BC, Canada

1998

"Keynote Address: The Emerging Keys to Success in European Retail Development," Innovations in European Retail and Entertainment Development conference, Urban Land Institute, Zurich, Switzerland

"Places & Spaces: Physical & Electronic," Digital Asset Management conference, University of Southern California, Annenberg Center for Communication, Marina del Rey, CA, USA

"The Jerde Partnership International: Current Work," Architecture and Environmental Design lecture series, California Polytechnic State University, San Luis Obispo, CA, USA

"1998 Honor Awards Recipient Panel," American Institute of Architects convention, American Institute of Architects, San Francisco, CA, USA

"Designing Multi-use Communal Places Worldwide," Harvard University, Graduate School of Design, Cambridge, MA, USA

"Leisure Entertainment—Strategic Placemaking," Leisure Property in Europe conference, International Quality & Productivity Center, Barcelona, Spain

"Jon Jerde," Southern California School of Architecture, Los Angeles, CA, USA

1997

"Top Entertainment Architects and Designers Sound Off," panel discussion on Urban Entertainment Development: The Secrets of Success, Urban Land Institute, Beverly Hills, CA, USA

"Urban Revitalization: Entertainment," panel discussion at the annual CRA conference and exposition, California Redevelopment Agency, Long Beach, CA, USA

"Asian Urbanization: Continuity + Transformation," panel discussion at the third Harvard Asia Pacific Design conference, Harvard University, Graduate School of Design, Cambridge, MA, USA

"Reinventing the Mall—The Entertainment Retail Revolution," breakfast seminar series, Deloitte & Touche, Century City, CA, USA

"The Architecture of Visceral Reality," International Design Conference, Aspen, CO, USA

"Jon Jerde and Eddie Wang: Experiential Design and Place-Making Worldwide," Harvard University, Graduate School of Design, Cambridge, MA, USA

"Jon Jerde, Architect—The Jerde Partnership International, Inc.," TED Technotainment conference, TED Conference, New York, USA

"Leisure Entertainment—Strategic Placemaking," Leisure Property in Europe conference, International Quality and Productivity Center, London, UK

"Playground of Dreams: Las Vegas and Beyond," Chicago Humanities Festival, Chicago, IL, USA

1996

"Q&A with Miller, Jerde, Swinney, Green, Sealey and Gannes," TEDSell conference, TED Conference, Monterey, CA, USA

"The creation of the world's largest computer-driven light show—The Fremont Street Experience, Las Vegas," Business Breakfast meeting, Pacific Design Center, Los Angeles, CA, USA

"Design in Asia: Theory and Education panel," Harvard University, Graduate School of Design Asia, Cambridge, MA, USA

"Hotel of the Future," design jury, American Institute of Architects, Washington, DC, USA

"Retailing and Entertainment: year 2000 AD," CB Commercial panel, International Council of Shopping Centers, Las Vegas, NV, USA

"Jon Jerde and Eddie Wang: Experiential Design and Place Making Worldwide," Harvard University, Graduate School of Design, Cambridge, MA, USA

"Place Making in Retail," Shopping Center Game conference, University of California at Los Angeles, Los Angeles, CA, USA

1995

"Shopping center design: Cost-effective and value-added approaches," International Council of Shopping Centers, Vienna, Austria

"The art of placemaking and its role in retail complex design with Jon Jerde and Eddie Wang," Harvard University, Graduate School of Design, Cambridge, MA, USA

"Horton Plaza and Fremont Street," symposium on Urban Theatre, "A New Urban Paradigm Rising in Las Vegas?", University of Nevada at Las Vegas, College of Architecture, Construction Management and Planning, Las Vegas, NV, USA

"Casinos: Playing the urban entertainment card beyond Las Vegas," conference on Developing Urban Entertainment Destinations: The Sequel, Urban Land Institute, Beverly Hills, CA, USA

"The art of place making: Its role in the retail complex," American Institute of Architects, Denver chapter, Denver, CO, USA

1994

"Current Work," one-day program about Creativity, Creative Projects and their Creators, University of California at Los Angeles, Interior & Environmental Design Program, Department of the Arts, Los Angeles, CA, USA

Keynote Address, 1994 Mid-Winter conference, International Downtown Association, Sacramento, CA, USA

"The container as the commercial," Westweek 1994, Pacific Design Center, Los Angeles, CA, USA

"Masterplanned community 2000," 1994 Spring meeting, Urban Land Institute, San Diego, CA, USA

"How developments like CityWalk, Horton Plaza and Mall of America will affect future planning of our cities," American Institute of Architects, Central Arizona chapter, Phoenix, AZ, USA

"The Art of Placemaking and its role in retail complex design with Jon Jerde and Eddie Wang," Harvard University, Graduate School of Design, Cambridge, MA, USA

"Reinventing the regional mall," International Council of Shopping Centers, Toronto, Canada

1993

"LA architecture comes of age," Interior Design program, University of California at Los Angeles, Los Angeles, CA, USA

"Jon Jerde," ArchiLECTURE series, Lawrence Technological University, College of Architecture and Design, Southfield, MI, USA

"Universal CityWalk," Universal CityWalk Forum Event, Architectural Guild, University of Southern California, Los Angeles, CA, USA

"Wave of the '90s: expansion and renovation," Powered-Up Spring convention, International Council of Shopping Centers, Las Vegas, NV, USA

"Focus on the future—a new direction," Urban Group conference, The Urban Group of Cambridge, Toronto, Canada

"Current Work," American Institute of Architects, Alabama Council, Montgomery, AL, USA

"Retail complexes: The art of experiential design with Jon Jerde," Harvard University, Graduate School of Design, Cambridge, MA, USA

1992

"Strategies for stabilization and growth in the '90s," Governor's Council on the Arts, Los Angeles, CA, USA

1989

"Shopping Centers: Strategies for Development, Operation and Investment," Advanced Study project, University of Pennsylvania, The Wharton School, Philadelphia, PA, USA

"Current Work," Alcan lectures on architecture, The Vancouver League for Studies in Architecture and the Environment, British Columbia, Canada

"Today's Images—a new excellence," Monterey Design conference, American Institute of Architects, California Council, Monterey, CA, USA

"Entertainment and Amusement in the retail concept," Spring meeting, Urban Land Institute, New Orleans, LA, USA

"Shopping centers: Strategies for development, operation, ownership and investment," University of Pennsylvania, Wharton School, Philadelphia, PA, USA

"Architects and the Pacific Rim," conference on Maximizing Profits/Minimizing Risks, Asian American Architects/Engineers Association, Los Angeles, CA, USA

"Commercial property trends: retail services," Harvard Real Estate Institute program, Harvard University, Graduate School of Design, Cambridge, MA, USA

"Student visions for architecture exhibit,"

honorary chair, American Institute of Architects, Los Angeles chapter, Los Angeles, CA, USA

"Larchmont proposal," September general meeting, Junior League of Los Angeles, Inc., Los Angeles, CA, USA

"33 D6 E6 Panel," Los Angeles Forum for Architecture and Urban Design, Los Angeles, CA, USA

"Outside and Inside: A history of visionary art and modernism," Scholar's conference, Los Angeles County Museum of Art, Los Angeles, CA, USA

Keynote Speech: "Synchronicity and the Human Condition," Faculty Retreat 1989, California State University, Northridge, CA, USA

"Placemaking: The New City for Universal City," Architecture Lectures and Exhibitions Fall 1989, University of California at Los Angeles, Graduate School of Architecture and Urban Planning, Los Angeles, CA, USA

"Creating places to be," Stadsmiljoradet conference, The Swedish Council for the Urban and Rural Environment, Stockholm, Sweden

1988

"Current Work," International Council of Shopping Centers, San Francisco, CA, USA

"The Future of Urban Retailing Centers," World Store '88 conference, The World Store Organization, Atlanta, GA, USA

"Center Environments as Experience and Attraction," Nordic Council of Shopping Centers, Copenhagen, Denmark

"Excellence in Retail Design," Las Vegas convention, International Council of Shopping Centers, Las Vegas, NV, USA

"Designs for Revitalizing Downtown," Planning and Developing Australian National conference, Royal Australian Planning Institute, Melbourne, Australia

"The Philosophy of City Revitalization," Creative City seminar, Victorian Ministry for the Arts, Melbourne, Australia

"Creating a quality city—giving the people what they ask for," City 1988 conference, Institute of Urban Development, Oslo, Norway

"Breaking the rules; the art of taking risks," 1988 Dialogue series, American Institute of Architects, Central Valley chapter, Sacramento, CA, USA

"Developing an urban quality of life," Evening Forum, Lusk Center for Real Estate Development, School of Urban and Regional Planning, Los Angeles, CA, USA

1987

"People and Architecture: Perspectives," Monterey Design conference, American

Institute of Architects, California Council, Monterey, CA, USA

"Architects on their designs for new downtown projects," Skyline 1990 Architecture Program, Friends of the Minneapolis Public Library and Downtown Council, Minneapolis, MN, USA

"Architectural design and historic preservation," Historic Preservation week, City of Phoenix Historic Preservation Commission, Phoenix, AZ, USA

"Retail development. What's new and exciting in Los Angeles and what's the arithmetic?," Fall meeting, Urban Land Institute, Los Angeles, CA, USA

"Urban design: evolving the public agenda," Not Yet Los Angeles conference, American Institute of Architects, Los Angeles chapter, Los Angeles, CA, USA

"Urban planning and design in the development process," Downtown Development conference, New York University, School of Continuing Education, New York, NY, USA

"The future of development—markets and products," conference on Toward 2000: The Future of Development, National Association of Industrial and Office Parks, Los Angeles, CA, USA

"An Evening with Jon Jerde," Society of Architectural Historians, Los Angeles, CA, USA

Keynote Address, the Centerbuild conference, International Council of Shopping Centers, Fort Lauderdale, FL, USA

1986

"Horton Plaza and the Economic Redevelopment of Downtown San Diego," US/Canadian Legislative Symposium, San Diego, CA, USA

"Scripting the City," lecture series on Patterns and Perspective: Planning for tomorrow's environment, University of Southern California, School of Urban and Regional Planning, Los Angeles, CA, USA

"Current Work," American Institute of Architects, Pasadena and Foothill chapter, Pasadena, CA, USA

"Making crucial development decisions," Real Estate Institute conference, New York University, School of Continuing Education, New York, NY, USA

"Scripting the City," Architectural Guild meeting, American Institute of Architects, Central Arizona chapter, Phoenix, AZ, USA

"Seventh Market Place," Downtown Breakfast Club, Los Angeles, CA, USA

"The Art of Selling Design to Sell: Horton Plaza," Professional Development Committee meeting, American Institute of Architects, San Francisco chapter, San

Francisco, CA, USA

"Humanism; the new theme of the '80s," 46th Annual meeting, American Diabetes Association, Inc., Alexandria, VA, USA

"Creating an instant environment with a design team," conference on The Challenge of Change, American Society of Interior Designers, New York, NY, USA

"Art in Architecture," Public Art Trust, San Diego, CA, USA

"The Retail Environment: a city within a city," IBD program, Institute of Business Designers, West Hollywood, CA, USA

"Current Work," Los Angeles 2000 Committee, Los Angeles, CA, USA

"Current Work," Anglo-American Real Property Institute, San Diego, CA, USA

"Making better use of urban space," Australian Institute of Urban Studies, Melbourne, Australia

"Landronics—The implications of information technologies for institutional structures regulating processes and urban developments," Asia Pacific conference series, The Lincoln Institute of Land Policy, Sydney, Australia

"Pedestrians in the grid," American Institute of Architect's Forum '86—Permagrid, Arizona State University and University of Arizona, Tempe, AZ, USA

1985

"Adaptive use/new use," mixed-use development seminar, Urban Land Institute, Washington, DC, USA

"Current Work," lecture program, The Architectural League, New York, NY, USA

"The Computer in a Finite World," Landtronics conference, Lincoln Institute of Land Policy, Los Angeles, CA, USA

"The International Stature of California Architecture and Design," lecture program, Pacific Design Center, Los Angeles, CA, USA

Keynote address: "The Revitalization of the inner city in the '80s and '90s, leading into the 21st century," Lambda Alpha, Northwestern University, Los Angeles, CA, USA

"Computers in urban and project planning," Landtronics conference, Lincoln Institute of Land Policy and Department of the Environment, London, UK

"Washington Street Mall," design awards program, American Institute of Architects, Indianapolis, IN, USA

"Current Work," lecture program, Institute of Store Planners, Los Angeles, CA, USA

"Environmental design for the 23rd Olympiad," 10th Annual Design Management conference, Design Management Institute, Massachusetts College of Art, Boston, MA, USA

"Architecture as urban design," University of California at Los Angeles, School of Architecture, Los Angeles, CA, USA

"Making cities work for people: an architect's view," Southern California Institute of Architecture, Los Angeles, CA, USA

"Updated shopping center and store design," conference, Associated Dry Goods Corporation, Fort Meyer, FL, USA

"Architecture and Art—Fantasy and Function," panel discussion, American Institute of Architects, California Council, Los Angeles, CA, USA

"People, places," lecture series on The Shape of Things, Fashion Institute of Design and Merchandising, Santa Ana, CA, USA

"Successful Downtown Malls," National Commercial Buildings exposition and conference, The Buildings Show, Dallas, TX, USA

"Completion competition: Hotel Intercontinental catalogue," design jury, San Diego Architectural Club, San Diego, CA, USA

"Current Work," County Growth seminar, Leadership Education Awareness Development, San Diego, CA, USA

"The Shopping Center Game in the '80s," conference, University of California at Los Angeles, Los Angeles, CA, USA

"Large buildings incorporating small jobs," Store Planning and Design conference, National Retail Merchants Association, New York, NY, USA

1984

"The American Urban Experience" and "The City of the Future," Centre City Development Corporation, San Diego, CA, USA

"Designing the Olympics," University of Southern California, Los Angeles, Los Angeles, CA, USA

"The Shopping Center Game in the '80s: Renovation and layout of shopping centers," symposium, University of California at Los Angeles, Los Angeles, CA, USA

"Santa Ana development potentials," Urban Land Institute, Washington, DC, USA

1983

"Your Turn/My Turn," 3rd Annual International Contract Furniture Design symposium, Pacific Design Center, Los Angeles, CA, USA

"Development of Horton Plaza, a case study," Urban Development, Mixed-Use Council Executive Group Meeting, Urban Land Institute, Seattle, WA, USA

"Project design and construction," Urban Waterfront Development conference, Urban Land Institute, Washington, DC, USA

"Horton Plaza, San Diego, California," Re-use of Land and Buildings conference, Royal Institute of Chartered

Surveyors, London, UK

"The Horton Plaza story," Urban Development, Mixed-use Council workshop, Urban Land Institute, Washington, DC, USA

1982

"1982 Honor Awards," design jury, American Institute of Architects, Pasadena and Foothill chapter, Pasadena, CA, USA

"The Shopping Center Game in the '80s: A practical approach," symposium, University of California at Los Angeles, Los Angeles, CA, USA

Exhibitions

1999

"Design Trends Exhibition," International Council of Shopping Centers, Las Vegas Convention Center, Las Vegas, NV, USA

"Idea Exchange Exhibition," International Council of Shopping Centers, Hyatt Regency Hotel, Long Beach, CA, USA

1998

"At the end of the Century: One Hundred Years of Architecture," Museum of Contemporary Art, Los Angeles. Traveling exhibition (1998–2001): Tokyo, Japan; Mexico City, Mexico; Cologne, Germany; Chicago, Illinois; Los Angeles, California; New York City, New York

"The 1988 Honor Awards exhibit," American Institute of Architects. Traveling exhibition from Washington, DC, to several AIA chapters

"Design Trends Exhibition," International Council of Shopping Centers, Las Vegas Convention Center, Las Vegas, NV, USA

1995

"100 projects/100 years," Pacific Design Center, Los Angeles, CA, USA

1994

"Tres Nuevos Simbolos para la Ciudad de Mexico," Museum de la Ciudad, Mexico City

"An Exhibition of Birdhouses designed and built by prominent Southern California architects," Pasadena Symphony Association, Pasadena, CA, USA

1986

"Jon Jerde: Redesigning the City," San Diego Art Center, San Diego, CA, USA

1985

"Transformations of Urban Spaces: Urban Theater," Pacific Design Center, Los Angeles, CA, USA

1999

"Interview with Jon Jerde," CNN Newsstand

1998

"Malling of America," interview with Saul Gonzales, KCET Life and Times

"Platinum Circle Awards," a video profile of Jon Jerde for the Hospitality Design Awards

"Current Work," a video lecture and slide presentation, Southern California Institute of Architecture (SCI-Arc)

1997

"Jon Jerde: The Architecture of Visceral Reality," video lecture, International Design Conference in Aspen, CO, USA

"Profile on Jon Jerde," radio interview, NPR Marketplace

1996

Appearance on Fox TV, "News at 10"

Appearance on CNN, "Showbiz Today"

1995

Interview with Laura Baxton, KUSI-TV San Diego

Appearance on CNBC News

1994

"Living on the Edge," video lecture, American Institute of Architects, Los Angeles chapter (AIA/LA) convention

"The History of Shopping Centers," documentary film by British Broadcasting Center (BBC)

"Virtually Las Vegas," documentary film by British Broadcasting Center (BBC)

"The Container as the Commercial," video lecture, Westweek 1994, Pacific Design Center

Interview with Charles Murphy, KABC News Saturday

Interview with Ron Tank, Turner Entertainment

Interview with Ruben Martinez and Pat Morrison, KCET "Life and Times"

1993

Appearance on ABC-TV network

1992

"Earth Talk," profile of The Jerde Partnership International by Yasuhiro Hamano

"The Fremont Street Experience," documentary film by Steenhoven Productions

1989

"Malltime," documentary film by 20th Century and Kai Productions

Appearance on ABC "Good Morning, America"

1988

Interview with Maria Shriver, CBS "Morning News"

Architect's acknowledgments

The passion, intelligence and persistence of a very large team of people have made this book, and the work it contains, possible. The process began when I invited a handful of talented individuals to join me in developing new ideas about citymaking. Eddie Wang, Charles Pigg, Paul Senzaki, Jim Campbell, William DeEiel, Alan Sclater, Ron Goetz and Trevor Thompson deserve special recognition as my first collaborators.

John Aleksich, Stan Hathaway, Brian Honda, Tim Magill, David Moreno, Glenn Nordlow, John Simones, Owen Tang and Joe Davoodzadeh have all been here since the 1984 Olympic Games changed the way the world viewed Los Angeles, and Horton Plaza transformed retail, entertainment and urbanism. They have shared my journey and I thank them for their talents and devotion.

Richard Orne, David Meckel, Scott Aishton, Norm Rosen, Fred DeNisco, Carl Worthington, Mark Lehner, Bob Cloud and Bob Reyes also contributed greatly to our early success.

Without the current intelligence and creativity of Rick Poulos, David Rogers, Paul Martinkovic, Arthur Benedetti, Ron Fiala, Mike Hong, Tom Jaggers, Bruce Jolley, Tammy McKerrow Poulos, Wasa Sakamoto, Curtis Scharfenaker, Mark Welz and Bob Woelffer, among many others, this firm would not be what it is today. I continue to be grateful.

Our co-creative working method has brought talented collaborators from all over the world to our Venice Beach offices. Those that deserve special thanks for their innovative contributions are Hank Hockenberger, Sussman/Prejza, Tamara Thomas, Emmet Wemple, Jeri Oka and EDAW, Joe Kaplan Lighting and Design, Mark Fuller, Jim Garland and WET, Selbert Perkins Design Collaborative, Jeremy Railton & Associates, Charlie White and OLIO and Robert Graham.

Beginning with Ernie Hahn over twenty years ago, we have worked with a distinguished breed of clients; individualists with strong points of view whom, nevertheless, supported us as we refined our concepts. We are honored to have worked with such enlightened groups as; the members of the Los Angeles Olympic Organizing Committee, especially Peter Ueberroth, Harry Usher and Dan Stewart; Lew Wasserman, Sid Sheinberg, Larry Spungin and Jim Nelson from MCA (now Universal Creative); Steve Wynn and Mirage Resorts, Inc.; Fremont Street Experience Limited Liability Company; Ing. Hans f.j. van Veggel and Multi Development Corporation; Kazuhiko Enomoto and Fukuoka Jisho Co., Ltd.; Kenichi Toh and Fukuoka Japan; Urban Design & Development Co., Ltd.; Melvin Simon and Herb Simon, Simon DeBartolo Group; Richard Green, Westfield; Lee Wagman and Trizec Hahn; and many talented others to create richer, more human places.

The opportunity to work with a publisher with the standards and discipline of Phaidon is truly a gift. Special thanks to Frances Anderton, a talented journalist who has understood our work and its implications from the outset, and to Craig Hodgetts, Margaret Crawford and Norman M. Klein for their provocative essays—I have learned from their diverse points of view. Thank you also to the Phaidon team: Karen Stein, Kim Colin, Iona Baird, Stuart Smith and Paul Hammond. Your diligence and expertise have delivered the kind of book that continuously places Phaidon at the top of the list.

Many in the firm have made valuable contributions to the making of this book, especially Anne Matranga, Stephanie Smith, Ralph Yanagawa and Judi Skalsky.

I have been fortunate over fifty-plus years to encounter a staggering number of people who have encouraged me to carve out and act upon my vision. Thank you to my mother and father, my wife Janice Jerde, my children Jennifer, Christopher, Maggie, Kate and Oliver Jerde, also to Cheryl Barnes, Bob Kramer, Ray Bradbury, Paolo Soleri (for letting me sleep under his drafting table when I was 15 years old) and Bob Irwin.
Jon Jerde

Editor's Acknowledgments

I would like to thank David Jenkins and Phaidon for agreeing that the Jerde Partnership would be a good subject for a book; Kim Colin for picking up the ball and running with it; Iona Baird for steadfastly shepherding it to completion; Ray Bradbury, Margaret Crawford, Norman M. Klein and Craig Hodgetts for endowing it with their intellectual brilliance and vitality; Stephanie Smith, Judi Skalsky and others at the Jerde Partnership for being such a pleasure to work with; Jon Jerde for being Jon Jerde; John Chase for being my constant sounding-board; my parents for the same thing, and for accidentally visiting Horton Plaza and loving it, thereby convincing me I was on the right track.
Frances Anderton

Photographic Acknowledgments

All visual material supplied by the architects unless otherwise stated. Photographic credits are listed where possible. The publisher will endeavor to rectify any inadvertent omissions.

t = top, b = bottom, l = left, r = right, c = center

Bildarchiv Foto Marburg: p.188cb;
Tom Brouwer: p.8bc;
Carla Breezer: p.75tr;
Dixi Carillo: pp.150, 152, 155bl, tc, tr;
Benny Chan: pp.40, 41, 42 bl, bc, br;
Mssrs P+D Colnaghi & Co Ltd: p.191;
Tom de Rooij Fotografie: pp.8bl, 161;
Christopher Dow: pp.75 bc, 86, 87;
EDAW: p.202;
Esto/©Norman McGrath: pp.48cr;
Joel Finler Collection: p.116tl;
FJUD: p.171 tr;
Gensler/M. Lorenzetti: p.15;
Tim Griffith: p.155c, bc;
Lawrence Halprin & Associates: p.48tl;
Karen Halverson: pp.76–77;
Robert Harding Picture Library: p.112br;
Robert Harding Picture Library/© Nigel Blythe: p.16tl, uc;
Robert Harding Picture Library/Nigel Francis: p.188br;
Robert Harding Picture Library/©Tom Mackie: p.116bc;
Robert Harding Picture Library/© Mike Newton: p.19tl, 120tl;
Robert Harding Picture Library/© Adam Woolfit: p.12bl;
Robert Harding Picture Library/© Paul Van Riel: p.191ct;
Itsuko Hasegawa Atelier: p.16lc;
Tim Hursley: pp.20tl, 138, 143;
Index, Firenze: pp.115c, 116tc,120cl;
Index, Firenze/Baldi: p.188cr;
The Jerde Partnership International: pp.15tr, br, 19bc, 23bc, 24c, 28tr, 29, 36, 37, 38, 51r, 52br, 56, 58, 59, 60, 62, 63, 64–65, 66, 68, 69, 70, 71, 74b, 78, 80, 81, 84, 85, 88, 90, 91, 92, 94, 95, 96–97, 100, 101, 102, 103, 108, 110, 111, 115tl, cl, bl, 124, 125, 128, 139, 146, 148, 149, 152, 153, 158, 164, 165, 166, 172–73, 176, 183tr, 192, 194, 195, 196, 198, 199, 200, 203, 204, 206, 207, 208–9, 210, 212, 213, 214, 215, 216, 217, 218, 220, 221;
The Jerde Partnership International (Jon Adams Jerde): pp.19br, 20c, 51cr, 55cr, cb, 81tl;
Hiroyuki Kawano: pp.11 b, 15cb, 23bl, 55bl, 116 c, 162, 165tr, 167, 168, 169, 170, 171tl, bl, br;
Dennis Keeley: p.11cb, 19 tr, 140, 141, 142, 144–45, 177, 178–79, 180, 181, 182, 183tl, bl, c, br, 185tr, 186–87;
Balthazar Korab: pp.12c, 44cl,bl,cr,br, 48bl, 191cl;
Charles Le Noir: pp.15 tl, 23cl, cr, 34, 55 tl, 75 tl, bl, c, 122, 126–27, 136, 174, 184–85;
Bonnie Lewis: pp.119br, 139 tl;
Barbara Malter: p.188tc;
©Norman McGrath: p.104;
Courtesy, The Museum of Modern Art, New York: p.16br;
Sam Nugroho: p.72;
Courtesy Cesar Pelli +Associates/Arthur Golding: p.47cr, br;
Peter Renerts: pp.11 tc, 104, 105 tl, 106–7;
Christian Richters: pp.23 tl, 156, 159, 160
©RTKL/Richard Watkins: p.15cl;
Scala Foto: p.112c;
Simmons/Del Zoppo Photographics: p.11 cl, tc, 26, 30–33, 51 cb, 129 c
Stephen Simpson: pp.8br, 15tc, 42, 43 tc, tr, 51cl, 52tc, 116bl, 129tl, tr, 133bl;
Doug Slone: p.55tl;
Eric Staudenmaier: cover, pp.115 tr, 119cr, 129 br, 130–31, 132, 133tr, 134–35, 188bl;
Tim Street-Porter: pp.8tc, c,12tc, cr, 20cl, 44tc, 52cl, tr, 119tr;
Sussman/Prejza: pp.28b, 51c;
Shin Takamatsu Architects + Associates: p.16bl;
Dauna Whitehead: p.24c